The Receptivity Project

The Receptivity Project

MAKE THE CONNECTION

Leslie N Bank

ISBN: 1507723024
ISBN 13: 9781507723029
Library of Congress Control Number: 2015901340
CreateSpace Independent Pub. Platform, North Charleston, South Carolina

This book is dedicated to the loving memory of my mother, Norma Beth Flom Bank.

Acknowledgments

would like to thank my parents, Jerry and Marsha Bank, and the rest of my family and friends for their unconditional love and support. I also want to acknowledge and give great thanks to my mentor and friend, Mary Devika Jones, to whom I owe much for coaching me and supporting my efforts. This book would not have been possible without direction from my spirit guides and their desire that I share these techniques with others. Finally, I want to thank Louann Pope for her dedicated editing of this book.

Table of Contents

Introduction · xi

Chapter 1   Balancing Your Energy · 1

Chapter 2   Energy 101 · 7

Chapter 3   Energy Signatures · 11

Chapter 4   The Physical Body · 15

Chapter 5   The Mind and Emotions · 21

Chapter 6   The Spiritual Body · 31

Chapter 7   External Toxic Influences · 37

Chapter 8   The Language of Spirit · 43

Chapter 9   Physical versus Extrasensory Perception · · · · · · · · · · · · · · · · · · · 49

Chapter 10 Being Persistent · 53

Chapter 11 Visualization Exercises · 59

Chapter 12 Fusing Auras · 69

Chapter 13   Detaching from Expectations· ·73

Chapter 14   Past Lives ·77

Chapter 15   How Your Life Fits Your Objectives ·81

Chapter 16   How Others in Your Life Assist You ·87

Chapter 17   The Trajectory of Your Life· ·91

Chapter 18   Ego versus Soul· ·93

Chapter 19   Levels of Spirit· ·97

Chapter 20   Messages from Spirit ·101

Chapter 21   Everyday Messages ·105

Chapter 22   The Dimes ·111

Chapter 23   Religion versus Spirituality· ·115

Chapter 24   A Channeled Message for You ·119

Chapter 25   Workbook ·123

            Bibliography ·127

Introduction

You are an amazingly intuitive person. How do I know this? Because everyone has intuition. A basic survival skill, intuition keeps us safe by alerting us to danger and giving us clues about how to remain safe. Intuition is always interacting with us, scanning people, places, and situations to ensure our physical safety. Intuition is more important than what our eyes, ears, and less dominant senses tell us. Something may seem safe, yet that nagging feeling remains that all is not as it seems.

As we grow older, we are taught to ignore our intuition. We live in a pragmatic culture that values reason and logic. Information that cannot be validated, that is received from an unknown source, is devalued. Intuition is a word rarely used in conversation. People may say they have a funny feeling about something or they have a gut instinct, but they won't generally call it intuition.

Why is intuition such a charged word? It opens up the proverbial Pandora's Box that houses all that is not reasonable. Any information without basis in reason is not a comfortable subject. Many people would rather repeat something they heard from someone, reliable or not, than disclose an intuitive message. At least with gossip, the source can be traced.

The Receptivity Project invites you to turn on your intuition. There are many reasons your intuition may have been silenced, but it is usually that the human mind is not allowing the intuitive voice to be heard. Perhaps your intuition told you not to buy a certain house, but you did anyway because it was a steal. You later find out why it was sold for such a low price. Intuition is always available, yet it is often silenced by reason. In fact, intuition has no ulterior motive and can always be trusted over logic and reason. If you get an intuitive message about something, you should never ignore it. Release the need to know how or why, and trust that what your intuition is telling you is absolute truth. Your mind is running a different program and cannot always be trusted; your intuition has only your best interests at heart.

This book is designed to help you explore the mystical aspect of your life. You can engage with spirit as much or as little as you want. In other words, take what you want from this book and leave what doesn't interest you. You can use the recommendations from this book to simply balance your energy, or you can use them for their intended purpose of connecting you to your spirit guides.

Just as we are all intuitive, we all have the capability of connecting to the spiritual dimension. Some people are born into the range of vibration that allows them to receive messages from spirit easily: we call those people gifted or psychic. There is a shroud of mystery over the world of mediums, and in this book I intend to lift it. You can do the same work as mediums do. You have the same abilities they have. Many mediums spend their time charging their clients for readings rather than training them to understand the messages they receive every day. Make no mistake, you are now and have always been receiving messages from spirit. Spirit speaks in a manner different than we usually do, so this book is designed to help you understand the language of spirit. When you understand this language, you will see that there are no coincidences and your spirit guides are constantly working on your behalf.

Whether your intention is to simply balance your energy or to manipulate your energy to receive messages from spirit more readily, this book will guide you. To begin, you must understand basic energy principles. Spirit is a form of energy; we are energy housed in human bodies. To bridge that gap, you must understand the realm of spirit and their language.

There is nothing to fear from making your own connections with spirit. I have provided guidelines to keep you safely within the light that contains all that is beautiful. The day you connect to the light will be the most amazing day of your life. It will be worth any effort that it may require. I attempted to channel for a year before my first breakthrough. Now it's as easy for me as turning on a light switch. It has been a journey to get where I am now, but I know I'm where I'm supposed to be.

Having access to spirit routinely makes my life easier. Today my spirit guides instructed me to call ahead to see if my coworker still wanted to meet. I followed this guidance and called him. As it turns out, he had forgotten our appointment and needed to reschedule. This guidance saved me an hour and a half of driving and wasted energy on this unnecessary trip.

How would knowing your life's purpose affect your life? Would you like to have access to information that can assist you in your everyday life? If you want to enrich your life beyond measure, then engage in The Receptivity Project. I was given the name and logo of this book in a channeling session. My spirit guides want me to reach as many people as I can with this important message:

Anyone can channel, and I can show you how.

CHAPTER 1

Balancing Your Energy

You know when your energy feels just right. When it's at an optimal level for you, you feel in the zone and like you can accomplish your goals. When your energy is either too high or too low, though, something feels off. You either feel like you don't have enough energy to make it through the day or you feel so much anxiety that it may distract you and prevent you from having a focused, productive day.

Some people have chronic imbalances that require a doctor's care and medication. If you are bipolar or suffer from depression or anxiety, continue to work with your doctor and take your medication. You can still use the strategies outlined in this book to assist you in gaining balance.

You can balance your energy through external influences that appeal to each of your five senses. I recently balanced myself by using a combination of dairy, soothing music, and a vanilla candle. This combination not only assisted me in relaxing but it also assisted a guest who joined me later.

Let's first talk about your sense of hearing. It's quite easy to change the radio station or adjust your digital music selection to a choice that will suit your mood. If your energy is already where you want it to be, then simply select something that you enjoy. If you are anxious or require calming, listen to New Age or slow music. The artist Enya is always my choice for calming, followed by Josh Groban or another soothing musical artist. If your energy is lagging and you want to be invigorated, put on a fast-paced selection such as hard rock. There's a reason they don't play Enya's music at spinning classes and aerobics classes–they want you to pace yourself to the music. Fast-paced music will always make your heart beat faster, and the rest of your physiology will follow.

Your sense of smell is a subtle but significant influence on your body. We have all had the experience of not feeling hungry until we smelled a delicious meal. Scents will imprint on your psyche: the smell of an ex-lover's cologne or the soup your mother used to make will instantly remind you of the memory. Your olfactory sense is a powerful game changer for your mood. I use essential oils and high-quality candles to assist me with energy management.

I typically require calming scents rather than invigorating scents, and my favorites are lavender, vanilla, almond, and coconut. I use these scents in the forms of body wash, colognes, essential oils, and candles. The essential oils should be good-quality oils from your local organic store and should be burned in a tea light holder with an oil reservoir. Candles should also be high quality or the negative effects may outweigh the positive effects.

My favorite invigorating scents include eucalyptus, orange, and other citrus. When beginning the day, I check in with myself to gauge my energy level. If it feels perfect, I just use my favorite body wash and cologne. If I need to calm myself, I might use vanilla body wash and vanilla cologne. If I need a bit more energy, I use peppermint or citrus body wash and citrus cologne. These scents stay with me throughout the day, assisting me with mood management.

Our most powerful sense is sight. Wearing bold colors will help ramp up your energy. Red is a particularly powerful, *grounding* color because it is associated with an energy center below your waist. Wearing muted, soft colors will calm your energy throughout the day. Clutter in your home, your car, or your work area will negatively affect your energy and mood. Take time to remove trash from your car and straighten your workplace area. I am often surprised at the state of people's cars, where many spend at least an hour a day. No matter how old your car, its interior should be clean and uncluttered. The exterior is not necessarily as important to your overall mood—that depends on your personality.

Your home is your sanctuary. When you return to your home, do you feel good or bad about it? If your response is negative, try to identify the reason. If you just need to cut the grass, take care of it. Since I began this chapter, I realized that I needed to follow my own advice. I bought an herb wreath for my front door. This wreath has improved the appearance and energy of my home's gateway by giving it a more hospitable feeling. Fresh flowers can be either calming or stimulating, depending on your selection. I enjoy buying flowers for myself and find that a vase of fresh flowers makes the harsh winter seem a bit more pleasant.

Once inside, how does your home feel? I encourage you to learn about feng shui principles for balancing the energy of your home. Feng shui is an ancient Chinese system of creating balance and harmony in your home through the placement of objects. This balance of energy should appeal to your sense of sight and foster harmony for anyone who enters your home.

Balancing through your sense of touch requires a bit more planning. There are some hands-on healing modalities, such as Rolfing, that are invigorating. Most massages, however, are intended to create a sense of calm. A session with a Reiki practitioner would be ideal for balancing, since that is the intended purpose of Reiki, an alternative medicine that originated in Japan. The name Reiki can be broken into two Japanese words: *rei* meaning "from above" and *ki* meaning "energy" (which has also been translated into "life force"). Reiki releases blockages in your energy system and facilitates energy movement.

Exercise can be either calming or stimulating. If it accelerates your heartbeat, it's invigorating. Aerobic exercises, such as running, biking, and swimming, are generally stimulating. Yoga, walking, and other slower activities can be calming. However, talking on your mobile phone while walking will negate any calming effect. Walking with headphones piping in music can be calming if the music is soothing. If the song is fast paced, the calming effect will be lessened. Walking in the woods is particularly calming and has a grounding effect.

A warm bath or shower can also have a calming effect. A cold shower has the opposite effect—it will stimulate your energy in an abrupt manner.

Meditation is the best way to experience tranquility. If you remove all stimulation or interruption and sit in stillness, you can eventually attain calmness. Meditation does not have to be done in a lotus position, and there is no technically correct way to meditate. Sitting in your car with your eyes closed, even while waiting for an appointment, can be very calming and provide you with a sense of relief.

We are surrounded by many types of stimulation. When I go to the mall, I am amazed at the number of smells there. Some stores distribute strong scent within, and the scent flows outside the store. There are also the scents of the pretzel stand, the pizza stand, and the cookie stand. Because I am particularly sensitive to smells, I find the mall unpleasant and limit each visit to a specific agenda. In addition to the smells constantly confronting me, there is noise and sensory overload in general. Most teenagers today seem to require two types of media at once: texting while watching television or some other type of multitasking. In Western society we are bombarded with stimulation. I recommend that you remove yourself from the constant digital stream by meditating or simply turning off your phone. I know that's a shocking thing to suggest, but you can do it!

The last physical sense that can assist you with balance is your sense of taste. All foods that originate from a source nourished by the sun are invigorating. Fruits, vegetables, and nuts all fall into this category. Foods derived from sources nourished by the earth, such as meat and dairy, are grounding foods. Foods that are far from their original form, such as processed foods packaged in a box or can, have a more negative effect. They can't give us life energy, because they do not come from a life form.

Caffeine has a stimulating effect; however, you may feel worse after it's worn off. Caffeine affects people differently; if you know you can use it in a healthy way, it's worth trying. Doctors constantly try to assess the health benefits of caffeine. Currently, one to two cups of coffee per day are said to have no known adverse health effects. Conversely, there are many calming teas on the market. These are commonly marketed as *bedtime teas* and include chamomile tea.

Your local health store will undoubtedly have an array of dried herb supplements to assist you in balancing your energy. I use Saint-John's-Wort in the winter months to lift me up and Valerian Root to assist me with calming and sleeping. Most organic stores have an herb consultant so ask for assistance if you have any questions or require advice.

All energy management begins with an assessment of your current state and a goal for where you want to be. Internal influences on your energy can be just as important as external ones. Managing your thoughts can help raise your energy level. Positive thoughts will assist you to an overall sense of well-being. Helping others, praying for others, and focusing on gratitude and love are all activities that will leave you feeling better in general.

The following Energy Balancing Chart provides a summary of how to use each of your five physical senses to balance your energy.

Energy Balancing Chart

Sense	Method	Stimulating	Calming
Hearing	Music, meditation, and silence	Rock or fast-paced music	Soft, slow music, meditation, or silence
Smell	Oils and candles	Peppermint, eucalyptus, orange, or other citrus	Lavender, vanilla, almond, or coconut
Sight	Feng shui design and use of colors	Bold colors and fresh flowers	Soothing colors, an uncluttered environment, and fresh flowers
Touch	Massage, exercise, baths, and Reiki	Rolfing, aerobic exercise, and cold showers	Soothing massage, yoga, Reiki, and warm baths
Taste	Foods, teas, and herbs	Food sources nourished by the sun, caffeine, and Saint-John's-Wort	Food sources nourished by the earth, calming teas, and Valerian Root

Chapter 1 Plug-In Points

- Your energy is always in one of three states: perfectly balanced, too high, or too low.
- You can balance your energy by appealing to your five senses: hearing, smell, sight, touch, and taste.
- Music, scents, food, exercise, colors, and feng shui techniques can all be used to balance your energy.
- You can disconnect from technology and television to reduce stimulation and relax.
- Meditation is an excellent way to return to center and find your balance.

CHAPTER 2

Energy 101

Energy is everywhere around you. The book you're holding contains energy, the air you're breathing contains energy, and the food you eat contains energy. Energy is an element of all forms of matter.

Humans in general, and Western society in particular, have difficulty grasping the existence of something invisible to the eye. It has long been accepted that germs and bacteria, although not perceived with the naked eye, exist and can be harmful. Matter exists in different forms—solid, liquid, and gas—and most people understand that gases, although sometimes undetectable by any of our five senses, do exist.

Energy is like the invisible oxygen that you breathe, essential for your survival yet not acknowledged on a conscious level unless compromised or not present at all. Just like a lack of oxygen, a shortage of energy will adversely affect your health.

There are a few different ways to refer to a person's energy field. When one can see an energy field, it's referred to as an *aura*. Your vibration, or frequency, describes how your energy feels to both yourself and others. Musical notes can be associated with frequencies of energy. Lower notes correspond to lower frequencies of energy, and higher notes correspond to higher frequencies of energy. Musical compilations have been created to clear energy blockages based on harmony between musical notes and energy frequencies.

There are seven major energy centers in your body. The manner in which energy is distributed within these seven centers creates your energy signature. Your energy signature is unique to you, much like your fingerprints. The difference between an energy signature and your other characteristics is that, unless you are interacting with someone who sees auras, your energy is not visible.

People who can see auras describe the seven major energy centers in your body as spinning wheels. The word *chakra* means wheel or disc in Sanskrit. The chakras work together to form your energy system, much like your digestive organs work together to form your digestive system. The seven chakras are located from your feet up to your head, from lowest frequency to highest frequency.

Each chakra governs a specific type of energy, and the chakras work together to create your energy field. Information is stored within each chakra; the chakras contain a database of information about you and your life. Each chakra has a specific area of focus and thus contains a specific type of information.

The first chakra, the *root chakra*, stretches from the bottom of your spine to the bottom of your feet and is described as red in color. This chakra is your connection to Mother Earth. It stores information about your family and tribal or cultural beliefs, as well as your feelings regarding security and physical survival. It has the lowest frequency of the chakras.

The second chakra is called the *sacral chakra*, is associated with the color orange, and is located at your navel. This chakra governs sexuality and reproduction, connectedness with others, creativity, and manifestation. It has a slightly higher frequency than the root chakra.

The third chakra, the *solar plexus*, is the region located above your navel and is associated with the color yellow. This region stores information about an individual's self-esteem and ego. Your personality and personal power are associated with this area.

The fourth chakra, located in the center of your chest, is referred to as the *heart chakra*. It is associated with the color green, and is the area where love is stored. In fact, both loving and painful memories may be found in the fourth chakra. Almost everyone has some pain from unpleasant experiences stored here. Compassion, empathy, forgiveness, and unconditional love are components of a healthy and strong heart chakra.

The fifth chakra, the throat chakra, is associated with the color blue. This is your voice, your truth, and your personal expression. People with healthy throat chakras express themselves honestly.

The sixth chakra is referred to as the *third eye* or sometimes the *brow chakra*. It is located on your forehead and described as dark blue or indigo in color. It is the area associated with higher consciousness. An open third eye may receive messages from spirit in a visual format or knowing of information without a clear source. Intuition and imagination are such manifestations.

Finally, the seventh chakra is called the *crown chakra*. This chakra is seen as white in color. It is your connection to a higher power. Intuitive information primarily enters you from above, through the crown chakra, although it can enter through other chakras. An open and high-energy crown chakra has a strong connection to the spiritual world and the Supreme Being.

Information related to your soul's evolution will come from your spirit guides through your crown and third eye, because those chakras are closely linked in purpose and vibration. I believe that our crown opens quite a bit as we sleep, and I have received a great deal of information and ideas just prior to drifting off to sleep. This receptivity of the crown chakra is the reason our dreams are so important.

This is a very basic overview of the chakras and what they do. There are many books and websites devoted to chakras, and I encourage you to read more about them. If you find energy and chakras interesting, you may also enjoy a Reiki course. My first Reiki course helped me to become spiritually conscious. Understanding energy is important for a number of reasons but here are the two most important reasons that come to mind: 1) if you want to adjust your energy, it helps to understand the basic principles and 2) spirit is in energy form so understanding energy will help your communications with your guides.

Chapter 2 Plug-In Points

- Your body has seven energy centers called chakras: root chakra, sacral chakra, solar plexus, heart chakra, throat chakra, brow chakra (third eye), and crown chakra.
- Each chakra contains a different frequency of energy and is a database of information about you and your life.
- Your energy is distributed among your chakras in a unique way; the chakras form your energy field.
- Reiki is an alternative healing modality helpful for achieving balance. Learning Reiki techniques and practicing Reiki on others is good way to learn about energy.

CHAPTER 3

Energy Signatures

"How your energy is distributed shapes how you see the world."
~ SPIRIT AS CHANNELED BY LESLIE N. BANK

Your energy signature is your unique energy distribution though your seven major chakras. People whose energy is more heavily weighted in the lower chakras strongly identify with their family of origin and their cultural belief system. Work, financial success, security, and survival are most important to them. They typically find it difficult to adopt different beliefs and spiritual practices from those of their family of origin. If you're in this category, you may struggle with disclosing to your family your new path and the messages you're beginning to receive from spirit. Your challenges may include deciding for yourself what your beliefs are and what's important in your life. You also need to ensure that your work is in balance with your family and personal time. A healthy balance between work and home can be a challenge for you. A lower chakra person may be more likely to work too many hours and place too much emphasis on work related successes. If your energy is in balance, your work and family life are equally important to you.

If your heart chakra is your strongest energy center, you experience life through your heart. Feelings are most important to you. Your biggest challenge is to avoid becoming bitter or cynical, because having this chakra as your strongest can be a difficult path in life. The most positive aspect of heart chakra people is that when they are in balance, they have an inner beauty that radiates outward for all to see.

If you are crown-chakra focused, you identify strongly with your mind. You endlessly process with your mind, but you run the risk of disconnecting from your heart (or at least overriding your heart in favor of your mind). Your challenge is to control your mind and not allow it to control you. Due to the strong energy present in your crown, you have the greatest potential for channeling; however, you must clear your mind so you can receive. A crown chakra out of balance results in a mind that streams messages constantly. A crown-chakra focused person who has a blockage, however, typically suffers from headaches, sometimes even migraines. Such a person will benefit from a meditation practice and from engaging in other grounding exercises and behaviors to balance his or her life.

A crown chakra out of balance is like a NASCAR™ track full of cars flying around it at high speed. Your spirit guides are like a car in the pit, trying to find a break in the action to reenter the race. You must create space on that track, your mind, so your spirit guides can enter. There is no one who will benefit more from a meditation practice than a crown-chakra focused person. Learning how the mind works and managing your mind are essential to balancing the crown chakra.

How your energy is distributed, your energy signature, is the most important aspect of your physical form. In my experience, people typically fall into one of two categories: energy strongest below the waist and energy strongest above the waist. When you learn more about your own energy and how it is distributed, you'll better understand your energy baseline. Each energy compilation has an out of balance shadow side associated with it. Where your energy is weighted most heavily can be a burden if the energy of the opposing chakras does not provide some sense of equilibrium.

Your health and your energy are so closely related that it is difficult to distinguish which is the cause and which is the effect. Did you get sick because you were exposed to germs or because you depleted your energy? You got sick because you depleted your energy, causing your body to be run down and unable to fight off the germs. A healthy energy field is the most important factor in your physical health. To understand the energy field's importance, know that you are comprised of energy that will endure long after your body is in the ground.

If you want to connect with spirit, you must take care of your body and your energy field. Your energy field has three components: physical health, emotional or mental health, and spiritual health. A deficit in one is enough to adversely affect the other two; the three are interdependent.

Chapter 3 Plug-In Points

- People whose energy is strongest below the waist are considered to have grounded energy; people whose energy is strongest above the waist are considered to have ungrounded energy.
- How your energy is distributed is the most important aspect of your physical body.
- Beyond your physical body, you also have an emotional or mental body and a spiritual body.
- Your three bodies are interdependent.

CHAPTER 4

The Physical Body

What you eat has a huge effect on your body and your vibration. There are only two real types of food: foods derived from organisms nourished by the sun and foods derived from organisms nourished by the earth. This real food does not include processed foods that come in a box, a can, or a frozen package. As I said earlier, these food sources cannot give life-force energy because they did not come from life. I am not referring to nutrition when I speak about these food sources—I am only referring to the effect of food on your vibration.

Foods that come from sources nourished by the earth include all animals (meat) and their by-products such as dairy. These foods lower, or ground, your vibration. When energy is disproportionately distributed in your upper chakras, you may feel emotionally unstable, irritable, easily provoked, unable to slow your thoughts, forgetful, or just distracted. You have these feelings because there is a disproportionate amount of energy in your heart, throat, third eye, and crown chakras. Eating a cheeseburger can remedy that feeling of unsettledness and inability to focus. Meat has a grounding effect on your energy field—its introduction into your body will pull some of that energy down into your lower chakras. This will adjust your vibration to a level that feels more functional.

Eating tubers or other root vegetables may also affect your frequency; it will ground people who have a very high vibration but will have a more neutral effect on people who already have a lower vibration.

On the other end of the spectrum from a diet focused on meat and dairy, a diet of raw food is associated with the highest vibration. Raw-food diets focus on raw fruits, vegetables, and nuts. Tropical raw foods have the highest vibration of all, because their origin is a place extremely close to the sun. These foods get their nutrition from the sun, so eating them will raise your vibration. Cooking vegetables impairs their ability to raise your vibration. I realized this by accident when I was eating a raw-food diet during my early attempts at channeling. That was when I made my first breakthrough.

Raw food puts you at the high end of your vibrational range. This diet should only be used if your energy is strongest below the waist. To raise your vibration, adopt a raw-food diet for several days to release all of the lower-vibration foods from your body. You will notice that you feel lighter in every way. Eating a raw-food diet will pull the energy from these high-vibration foods into your upper chakras and adjust your energy to an optimal level.

You should experiment with food to see how various foods make you feel. Become conscious of what you put in your mouth and its effect on your body. People with grounded energy should adopt a diet that will raise their vibration. People with upper chakra energy should adopt a diet that will lower their vibration.

Another way to ground is exercising outdoors. It is particularly helpful if you can walk in the woods or on a path enveloped by trees. If you are feeling very ungrounded, a barefooted walk on grass or the beach will benefit you. When you draw the earth's energy up through your feet, it has a grounding effect. Any connection with nature typically has a calming and therefore grounding effect. Other activities that have a calming, or grounding, effect are yoga and tai chi. It varies—my upper-chakra-oriented friends find the beach grounding, but I require trees to feel a truly grounding effect.

The recommended formula for chakra balancing is to use grounding methods for people who have stronger energy within their fifth, sixth, and seventh chakras and to use invigorating methods for people who have stronger energy within their first, second, and third chakras. People who are strong in the fourth chakra are somewhat in the middle of the spectrum, but their energy will be stronger on one side or the other. I have performed Reiki on one woman who is strong in the fourth chakra but very balanced on both sides; however, in my experience this configuration is not typical. Refer to the Energy Balancing Chart in chapter 1 for techniques to manipulate your energy until you feel a sense of balance.

One way to gauge your energy distribution is to use Ayurvedic principles. Ayurveda is a holistic, ancient Hindu medical science that associates *doshas* (body types) with elemental energies and stresses that balance among the three is required for optimal health. The three doshas are *Kapha* (elements of water and earth), *Pitta* (elements of fire and water), and *Vata* (elements of air and space).

Ayurvedic doctors believe that every person has one or two dominant doshas and that energy is distributed among all three doshas in a manner unique to the individual. The work of renowned medical doctor, speaker, and best-selling author Deepak Chopra has helped to introduce the philosophy of Ayurveda to Americans. His website (www.deepakchopra.com) offers a plethora of opportunities for growth, healing, and insight.

I believe that your Ayurvedic dosha will correspond to your energy distribution. If you are Kapha dosha, your energy is grounded (earth) and concentrated in the lower chakras, one through three. If you are Pitta, your energy is concentrated in the middle (fire) or heart chakra, the fourth chakra. If you are Vata, your energy is strongest in your head (air) in the fifth, sixth, and seventh chakras. You can find a dosha questionnaire on Dr. Chopra's website that will give you feedback about your doshas. From your doshas, you can infer your chakra energy distribution; they are correlated because they both describe your energy composition.

Other indications of where energy is stored in your body can be found in your lifestyle and personal characteristics. I have found that people who don't wear a watch usually don't possess grounded energy. If you toss and turn all night and can't turn off your mind, you are probably crown-chakra focused. If you are very successful in business, you may have a lot of energy concentrated in the root chakra. If you are very emotional, you are probably strongest in your heart chakra.

Rather than guess, however, you should consult a Reiki practitioner for feedback about your energy. Just like we don't accurately hear the way our voice sounds to others, it is nearly impossible to discern your own energy distribution. To be sure, you can obtain a Reiki practitioner's evaluation and an Ayurveda test. When you know your energy distribution, you can begin to adjust it. You may find recommendations for a Reiki practitioner at your local metaphysical store or organic market.

Substance use can affect your vibration. For example, caffeine, sugar, alcohol, tobacco, and narcotics all affect your vibration in varying degrees. Many people with high vibrations use tobacco to ground themselves without being conscious of it. Tobacco relaxes them, lowering their vibration and allowing them to function more easily in the grounded world. Understand, however, that I am not advocating tobacco use, with its well-documented side effects—I'm simply describing behavior. Narcotics are sometimes prescribed by a doctor. If your doctor has prescribed a narcotic medication for you, you should consult him or her before discontinuing your medication. Alcohol is considered socially acceptable, but usually just one glass of wine puts me out of range of spirit's messages. For me, caffeine is okay in moderation. If caffeine leaves you feeling jittery because you're sensitive to it, you may be too agitated to be functional, let alone receive spiritual messages. Sugar can have an effect on your energy field; too much sugar can also leave you feeling agitated.

The key here is that everyone is different; each of us has a unique energy distribution with a baseline and a range on both sides of that baseline. You can learn more about your energy baseline and how foods affect you by getting an energy analysis and then paying attention to your body and what affects it. Be mindful in your eating habits, and then mindful after eating, to discern any changes in how you feel.

Food nourished by the earth.

Food nourished by the sun.

Chapter 4 Plug-In Points

- Only two types of food can balance your energy.
- Food sources nourished by the sun, such as fruits, vegetables, and nuts, will raise your vibration.
- Food sources nourished by the earth, such as meat and meat by-products, will lower, or ground, your vibration.
- Food is a game changer for your vibration: it can quickly help you feel more balanced.
- Ayurveda is a holistic, ancient Hindu medical science that can provide suggestions for energy balancing.
- Use of substances such as caffeine, sugar, alcohol, tobacco, and narcotics can affect your vibration.
- When you find your energy balance point, you can use food and Ayurvedic principles to maintain your energy or to manipulate it higher or lower.

CHAPTER 5

The Mind and Emotions

Spirit's question in response to a concern: "Why do you worry?"
My response: "It's part of the human experience."
Spirit's response: "If you believe that to be true, then it's true."

ood and exercise definitely affect your body, but your mind is the computer that runs your body. The health of your chakra system (your energy field) is greatly influenced by your emotions. Your emotions are directly related to the meaning you attach to events, experiences, and thoughts.

For most of us in Western culture, our minds run a mile a minute and we feel we have no control over the direction or pace of our thinking. I remember the first time I was introduced to the concept that our thoughts create our emotions and we can control our thoughts. This happened when I read Dr. David Burns's book *Feeling Good*, which was first published in 1980. After reading his book, I began to reprogram my mind with messages that made me feel good rather than bad. I can't say that the bad messages never creep back in, but realizing that I have control has made a significant difference in my mental health.

The power of the human mind is amazing. All actions and manifestations in life are first a seed, or thought, sown in the mind. All matter begins in thought form. I believe Buddhism offers something for all of us in Western society. Buddhism is based on the teachings of Siddhartha Gautama, commonly known as the Buddha, which means "awakened one." The Buddha was born in India about five centuries before Jesus Christ's birth. His teachings are based, in part, on the belief that the human experience of suffering is optional. The Buddha has suggested a path to enlightenment and the cessation of suffering through loving detachment.

The basic principles of Buddhism are the following: be kind to all living beings, do no harm through word or deed, and accept life as impermanent. The Buddha believed that the need for safety and security in an ever-changing world caused humans needless suffering.

The Buddha taught that meditation is the best way to examine the mind and how it functions. If the mind can be conditioned to release its attachment to outcomes, expectations, and material possessions, suffering can end. The depth of thought expressed by the Buddha cannot be summarized in a paragraph or two. If you accept the concept that suffering is optional, you may appreciate the wisdom found in the Buddha's work.

Don't feel like you need to choose between Buddhism and your religion of practice (if you have one). Buddhism is more a philosophy and a way of life than a religion. You can practice both your own religion and Buddhism. Western culture could really benefit from Buddhist teachings right now.

I enjoy the writings and lectures of Pema Chodron, an ordained Buddhist nun, teacher, and author from Gampo Abbey, a Buddhist monastery located in Canada. Her Western roots enable her to explain the Buddha's messages in a manner I find easy to understand. Her website can be found at www.pemachodronfoundation.org.

Another author whose perspective I enjoy is Byron Katie. She encourages us to trace our emotional state to our thoughts and beliefs about a situation. Katie states that it is our belief about an issue—not the issue itself—that causes us pain. She teaches detachment in a unique way, and there is a peaceful message in her philosophy. Her web site (www.thework.com) offers free resources about what she calls *The Work*, which challenges the thoughts that cause you pain.

To master your mind, and therefore your thoughts, you must first become conscious of how your mind works. Monitor your mind without filter or purposeful direction. Merely observe how your mind jumps around from topic to topic, making judgments about other people and attaching meaning to everything you see. If you wear a watch with a timer, set it on an hourly chime, then, each hour when it goes off, ask yourself what you were just thinking about.

Regardless of whether Buddhism resonates with you, you will find it helpful to adopt a meditation practice. The purpose of meditation is to clear your mind of all thoughts and be still. If a thought pops into your mind—and it will—don't be upset with yourself. Dismiss the thought and return to a clear mind. Being awake without thoughts is very difficult to do, but if you can be the master of your mind rather than a slave to your mind you will be a happier person. Why? Because as the master, you decide what to feed your mind, and if you choose to feed your mind only positive and happy thoughts, your mood and emotions will reflect that.

Our lives all include stress or the opportunity for stress. What does that mean? I experience stress just like everyone else does, but, as spirit reminds me, stress and worry can be optional. Be conscious about your stressors, and decide if they are important enough to give them energy. Here is one example of unnecessary stress:

I once had a coworker who frequently called me during his hour-long commute from work to his home. I was amazed that nearly every time he would interrupt our conversation to scream at a motorist for some perceived discourtesy or infraction. He would get worked up during a tirade directed at someone who could not possibly hear him because they were both going at least seventy-five miles per hour with their windows closed.

After several opportunities to observe his behavior, I realized that driving home can be either a stressful and confrontational experience or a peaceful and centering one. It's a choice. How he responded to someone cutting him off or driving slow in the fast lane was his choice. And since there are always bad drivers out there—although we never consider that we may be one of them—every commute is ripe with possibilities for getting upset at the general motoring population.

I decided then that I would refuse to get angry over a traffic incident, slight, or situation. If someone cuts me off, I say to myself, "He must not have seen me. If someone wants to move over, I let them in. If someone tailgates me, I either ignore it or assess my speed and consider giving him or her the lane. I am now much more accommodating toward other motorists. I can't say that I've never violated this rule, but I have made this attitude a basis for my driving habits. If motorcyclists speed by me at over a hundred miles per hour, I say a prayer for them as they disappear down the road. If you are giving up energy and power because of any driving-related issues, I invite you to commit to this way of thinking for one week. You will not want to go back to your previous way of driving.

By reframing existing thoughts and releasing expectations, we can create a more peaceful reality for ourselves. The driving example is a relatively easy exercise. Visiting your in-laws might be a harder one, but you can use this framework for anything in your life that causes you to lose energy. Take a moment to consider what everyday situations cause you to lose some of your energy. Most of the time, we cannot change the situation, but we can change our response to the situation.

We think we know how things should be. We have expectations, and when things don't work out the way we'd hoped, we lose energy and power with resentment and anger. Judgment is one of the most pervasive and harmful thought processes and will always lower your vibration because it is associated with a lower level of energy. None of us like to be judged by others, yet we all engage in it ourselves. Whenever I recognize that I am judging, I try to dismiss the thought and say to myself, You're not in a position to judge him. You know nothing about him. I then assess what it is that I am judging and acknowledge I am uncomfortable with something within myself. Consciousness is the first step to change.

I was born in 1963 to a woman who already had three children who had been taken from her by the state due to her inability to parent. She ultimately had six children with five different men. I later learned that all of my half brothers and sisters born to my birth mother are substance abusers, have criminal records, or both. They have not had an easy life. The only difference between them and me is opportunity. I was adopted at birth by a loving couple that badly wanted a child. "There but for the grace of God go I" is definitely true for me—I could easily be the prostitute I see walking along the highway or the alcoholic mother of five on welfare. It was only because of God's grace that my parents adopted me at birth.

As a result, I do not judge those who have lesser circumstances, although there are other issues that I tend to judge about so I have to monitor those thoughts. We all have something, whether we are conscious of it or not, that makes us cringe when we see it. Knowing yourself and your trigger issues is the first step to changing your internal dialogue.

If you find yourself judging someone, try to replace this lower-frequency energy with love from your fourth chakra. Pray for the person, send loving energy to the person, and then release the judgment. We may never get to a place where there is no judgment within us, but we can try to recognize judgment, replace it with a higher-level emotion, and let it go. We can only try to do our best; we are all works in progress.

Another pattern that can lower your frequency and have many other negative effects on your body, psyche, and energy is the withholding of forgiveness. We all experience hurts and injuries inflicted upon us by family, friends, and even strangers. People tend to hold onto these hurts for a variety of reasons but mostly because they want to. From their perspective, they have been victimized in some way. But holding onto hatred, resentment, or anger because of a real or perceived emotional or physical wound does not serve your higher self. It keeps you trapped in the energy of the original injury. You are forced to relive that energy each time you reflect on the injury. Forgiving someone that has hurt you doesn't mean you are okay with what happened. It just means you're freeing yourself of a heavy burden and giving yourself the gift of peace.

Withholding forgiveness only hurts you—it does not hurt the person you are refusing to forgive. They are not suffering with this negative energy inside them—you are. They may not even be aware—or worse, they may not care—that you refuse to forgive them. The Buddha said, "Holding onto anger is like grasping a hot coal with the intent of throwing it at someone else; you are the one who gets burned."

I would like you to look within yourself and find someone in your life who has hurt you in some way and who you've had difficulty forgiving. Elevate your perspective; try to look at the situation in an objective way. What has this situation taught you, and what can you still learn from it?

Here is an example:

Consider a woman who has been married for twenty-five years. She is neither overly happy with her husband, nor is she unhappy. He pays the bills and is reliable, and she is content with her place in life. This man comes home one day and informs her that he has met another woman and is leaving her for the other woman. She feels numb as she watches him pack an overnight bag and walk out the door.

This woman has a choice. She can spend the rest of her life bitter about this development. She can choose to never love again, to never open herself up to this kind of hurt again. This doesn't sound like a good option, yet many people choose it.

A better scenario is one in which she works through her pain and finds healing. The path for her healing requires forgiveness. She lets go of the anger and resentment she felt toward the man who had said he would love her for the rest of her life, and she moves on. She experiences exponential emotional and spiritual growth due to her ability to weather this storm, and she emerges stronger than ever. Finally, she meets a man who suits her much more than her ex-husband had. She experiences a level of happiness she never thought possible; she truly feels as if husband number two is her soul mate.

In this scenario she managed to accomplish a life objective: to handle heartbreak and respond by learning to love again. Husband number one was *supposed* to leave her as part of a soul contract. He did what she had asked him to do so that she could grow and learn a painful but powerful lesson about love and healing. He did what he was asked to do and she did what she was supposed to do. This was an agreement that they had made before incarnating into this life.

The bottom line is this: Look at each of your wounds and consider its larger meaning. What is the higher interpretation of the experience? Remember that the path to healing requires forgiveness. You're not hurting anyone but yourself by nurturing old wounds. I recommend that you read *Radical Forgiveness: A Revolutionary Five-Stage Process to Heal Relationships, Let Go of Anger and Blame, and Find Peace in Any Situation,* by Colin C. Tipping. He speaks about the higher perspective, and I found his formula for forgiveness to be an effective approach. If you need to go to therapy to fully process the experience, then do so. I do not recommend an open-ended therapist relationship, however; go there with a time frame and goals in mind, and try to stick with them. Release the negative energy any way you can.

My best friend Jeanne Remington is a hypnotherapist in Jacksonville, Florida. She told me that it is possible, through hypnosis, for people to fully release all of the energy associated with an injury so that it has no further power over them. I believe that hypnotherapy is an insightful and powerful tool in the healing process. It can bring you closer to the spiritual issues associated with the injury, make you aware of any past-life relationships with the person involved, and cleanse you on a deep level. Consider hypnotherapy if you feel stuck in the process of forgiveness.

Another approach to releasing negative energy that no longer serves you is to ask spirit to show you how. One way I've found is to pray for the person you are having trouble forgiving. Even if the prayer comes from your head and not your heart, begin with that. Ultimately, you are saving yourself when you forgive. Forgiveness is an action that must be done if you're serious about your spiritual development and your overall health.

In addition to judgment and anger, other lower-level emotions are fairly obvious. They include jealousy and envy, which are the opposite of empowerment. If you want something that someone else has, you should examine how they achieved it and try to duplicate their efforts. The books *The Law of Attraction: The Basics of the Teachings of Abraham* by Esther and Jerry Hicks and *The Secret* and *The Power* both by Rhonda Byrne are guides to manifesting what you want. Focusing on what you don't have (but which someone else does) is not positive and will only reinforce the situation. If you engage in this negative reinforcement, you must flush it out of your thoughts (and thus your emotions) to raise your vibration and change your situation.

Fear is another lower-level emotion. Fear and faith cannot coexist, because they are opposites. I have met many people who go to church regularly and pray regularly yet suffer from deep-seated fear and anxiety. They truly love God and believe that God loves them, yet they can't give up the need to tightly control their lives. They don't seem capable of placing their troubles in the hands of a higher power.

I was told by spirit long ago that if we appear to have life under control, that's an illusion created by the ego. The reality is that we have no such control over anything other than perhaps what we eat for breakfast. Even that's questionable if your house suddenly catches on fire. These illusions created by the ego keep us from feeling the enormity of the universe and our small, powerless place within it. But fear of any type is simply a lack of faith. Fear will lower your vibration and may prevent you from feeling the joy inherent in your life.

The irony of fear is that people typically fear an event that has not yet happened and may never happen. By feeding the universe with your mind's energy and the image you attach to that fear, you may actually draw this person or event closer to you. The power of your mind may create exactly what you fear most. This is reason enough to expel fear from your life and replace it with faith and love. Your spirit guides have a greater plan for you and know what is best for you.

In addition to fear, other emotions that keep your frequency in a low state are frustration, hatred, guilt, despair, worry, and irritation. These emotions will all stand in the way of your joy in the present moment.

Many emotions serve to raise your vibration. The most powerful vibration changer is unconditional love. Pure love is the frequency of spirit. Love is the only true emotion; anything that is the opposite of love is not our purpose here. Our true purpose is to love everyone here on our planet, without exception, not just our families and communities. We are all connected; the illusion of separateness is created by the ego. Unfortunately, this illusion of separateness allows humans to commit horrific acts upon each other.

Great leaders such as Jesus, Mahatma Gandhi and Martin Luther King, Jr. have shown us that the true power of love is stronger than force. Replace judgment with love, replace resentment and hurt with love for yourself and your aggressor, replace jealousy and envy with love. Love is the answer to every spiritual question and will always triumph over darkness. It is always the path to peace. Love is the highest vibration. Fill your heart with love, and leave no room for anything else.

Joy is another experience that we should be enjoying regularly in our lives. It seems to me that most adults forget this aspect of themselves so they can fulfill their responsibilities to their work and family. The trouble is that many times they forget how to retrieve their sillier side when they do have time to play. Playtime is essential for all of us. Going to the gym doesn't count. I have many friends who are what I would describe as "big kids," and I love that about them. I believe my friends would say the same about me. Don't take life and yourself so seriously that you forget how to have fun.

Try to turn your mobile phone off when spending time with loved ones. Unless you work in a field that requires you to be available, ignore the phone sometimes. Your loved ones and friends need to feel that all of your energy is with them rather than with a box that constantly streams texts and e-mails. The box should support you, not the other way around. Taking the box with you when you are enjoying your free time may neutralize any positive effects of the activity. I am constantly amazed when I see people out on their daily walks but chatting on their mobile phones. The emotional and mental benefit of their walks may have been negated by the phone calls. Consider being out of reach for an hour or two. People will understand. If they don't, detach from their expectations.

Another internal issue that can affect your vibration is an imbalance of ego. Ego is a necessary element of life. Without it, we would probably still be living in our parents' basements, unshaven and playing video games all day. Ego gets us moving and helps us to create a life for ourselves. Excessive ego, however, is an over-identification with the self, and it generates lower-chakra energy. The opposite of ego is humility, which is always present in a grounded and balanced person.

To speak with spirit is an honor; keep in mind that these messages do not come from the receiver but rather from a higher source. A medium or psychic is merely a conduit, a channel. As you progress in your journey, always remember that the ego must not be allowed to take credit for anything. To be full of ego is the antithesis of a spiritual being.

Other emotions that will raise your frequency are all components of love: enthusiasm, passion, satisfaction, empathy, compassion, gratitude, excitement, and joy. Being in a continuously loving state will keep you in the frequency that allows contact with the spiritual dimension.

Relax, nothing is under control.

Chapter 5 Plug-In Points

- Your emotions are generated by your mind and the meaning you attach to events and situations.
- If you are not consciously controlling your mind, it is controlling you.
- Stress is optional.
- Buddhism is a philosophy from which all people can benefit; you can practice both Buddhism and your religion (you do not need to choose).
- Forgiveness frees you and raises your vibration.
- Difficult life situations all have lessons embedded in them.
- Any emotion within love's frequency will raise your vibration.
- Love is the frequency of spirit; feeling love and giving love will raise your vibration.

CHAPTER 6

The Spiritual Body

"You have no idea how powerful prayer is. Every prayer is heard."
~ SPIRIT AS CHANNELED BY LESLIE N. BANK

Aside from love, prayer is the most powerful way to raise your frequency. Prayer generates energy from your heart through either your mind or your fifth chakra, your throat. Whether silent or audible, all prayers are heard. Prayer must begin in your heart and be in your own voice. Reading a passage from a prayer book is not a prayer but rather a practice or a ritual created by the tribe. If you are reading a prayer from a book but thinking about getting home from church in time to watch the game, you may as well be reading the newspaper. I do not seek to offend those who find comfort in the church, but going to church is not necessarily a spiritual practice. Reading, singing, and socializing with others of like mind can supplement, but cannot replace, your own spiritual practice. A spiritual practice is one that engages your mind, heart, and soul with your higher power. Your conversation with your chosen Supreme Being must be in your voice and from your heart. Despite what some organized religions teach, you do not need them or their practitioners to act as a conduit between you and your higher power. You have your own direct line.

Once when I was lying in bed, a former police officer coworker who had been killed in the line of duty appeared to me. She looked beautiful, and there was an enormous amount of light behind her. I knew that she was in a marvelous place. She seemed so peaceful. She asked me to pray for her sister, whom I also know, and I told her that I would do so. She said, "You have no idea how powerful prayer is. Every prayer is heard."

In 2012, a sudden and severe thunderstorm hit the region in which I live, and twenty-two people were killed. Hundreds of others were without power. During the height of the storm, a large tree limb landed on my house's roof. I heard it hit and became concerned about the huge oak trees surrounding my house. I prayed that my son and I would be safe and that our house would not be damaged.

When I went outside the next morning to assess the damage, I saw that, although many leaves and twigs were scattered, with the exception of the one tree limb nothing had fallen from the trees. Both of my neighbors had suffered large tree-sized fallen limbs and would need to call a tree expert to clean up the mess. I had escaped that headache. I then looked up at the glass wind chimes hanging next to my side door—they were not chipped or cracked. I stared at them incredulously for a few seconds and heard, "The power of prayer." I knew that my prayer for protection had been heard and answered. I only wished that I'd thought to ask for protection for my entire neighborhood.

Prayers are always heard. They are not always answered in the manner that we would like, but they are heard. I would like you to begin the practice of a prayer list. It can be a list of people you know or don't know, love or hate. You will pray for these people each night before going to sleep. It's difficult to worry and toss and turn when you have taken the focus off yourself and placed it on others. I find that I usually don't make it to number five before falling asleep. If you find yourself falling asleep before you've finished your list, you may want to order your list by urgency. I suggest you include the following people in your prayer list:

- People you know who are sick, suffering, struggling, lonely, or in need of assistance
- At least one person you don't know (a homeless person you see every day, a family you saw on the television news, or a suffering person you heard about but have never met)

After you've adopted this practice and you feel ready, consider adding the following people to your prayer list:

- Someone you don't like
- Someone you are having difficulty forgiving
- Someone who looks different than you do

Here is an example of a prayer I say sometimes when I know I will be falling asleep quickly:

Lord, I pray that everyone on my street experiences good health, prosperity, and happiness. I pray that everyone within my zip code experiences good health, prosperity, and happiness. I pray that everyone within the state of Maryland experiences good health, prosperity, and happiness. I pray that everyone within the United States experiences good health, prosperity, and happiness. Finally Lord, I pray that everyone in the entire world experiences good health, prosperity, and happiness.

That covers it. It takes less than a minute. I began this prayer ritual when I was praying for two of my neighbors who had cancer. Then I began to pray for others on the street, and I eventually expanded the prayer to encompass the whole world. The entire world certainly needs prayer right now.

If I'm still awake, I usually pray for people I know who are sick or suffering in some way. I have a list of these people and when someone heals, I replace them with someone else. Sometimes I incorporate people back into my prayers. My cousin had lung cancer and has been in remission for several years. She was on my prayer list for at least two or three years, and I periodically thank God for her health and pray that she will remain healthy.

The following are not allowed in your prayer list:

- Material things
- Job promotions, success, lottery numbers, and so forth
- Revenge and other negative wishes

You may pray for yourself, but it is best to leave that for last. Prayer for yourself should be limited to urgent matters—for example, if you are in need of and are requesting healing.

Consider prayer a sacred time. During prayer you have your Supreme Being's ear, so ensure your prayer is worthy. He doesn't care if you ever get that corner office. That is not to say you can't use your mind power to acquire things that you want. I'm saying that the sacred dialogue of prayer is not the time to do so. What's the difference between praying for something material and trying to bring the material item to you with the power of your mind? When you pray for material things, you are asking spirit to assist you in acquiring them. When you use the power of your mind to bring material things into your life, you are using your own power and energy to create them. There are many books available for people who want to use their minds to create more for themselves. There's nothing wrong with that practice, but don't engage in it while praying.

Feeling a sense of gratitude will always elevate your mood and therefore your vibration. Gratitude can bring you more of what you want and always leaves you feeling better about your circumstances. Sometimes when it's freezing outside and I'm lying in bed listening to the wind howl, I consciously feel grateful to have a warm bed in a heated home. What do you take for granted because it's always been there yet you would miss immensely if you had to do without it? Right now I can easily say that's a refrigerator, which is being replaced by a new one to be delivered tomorrow.

Start your day with a gratitude "check-in" list of five things for which you are grateful. A gratitude practice will begin your day in a positive way. In addition, a sense of gratitude will bring more positive things into your life.

According to Jerry and Esther Hicks in their book *The Law of Attraction* and Rhonda Byrne in her book entitled *The Secret*, what we focus on increases in our lives. Be careful what your mind attaches to—your thoughts are energy and all physical matter begins in energy form. Feeling grateful is a good idea in and of itself, but the feeling of gratitude may cause your life to become filled with even more reasons to feel grateful. Gratitude fosters a positive cycle of abundance.

While I was a lieutenant with the Baltimore Police Department, I had the opportunity to provide favors—such as free parking at sporting events—for friends, family, and coworkers. One thing I noticed is that when you do something once for someone, they are grateful. If you do the favor regularly, over time they will become so accustomed to the treatment that they will expect it. In this case I got phone calls asking, "Did you get *my* parking pass for the stadium again this year?" The parking pass had become an expectation rather than a perk. This isn't a judgment but merely an observation, and it doesn't apply to everyone, but I believe that taking things for granted is human nature and therefore the way most of us operate. We only appreciate some things when they are suddenly gone.

It's easy to lose sight of the practice of gratitude in our daily lives. Take a moment each day to thank spirit for all that you have been given. My nightly prayers begin with a message of thanks to God. No matter how bad my day was, I thank God for it. I spent nearly twenty-five years as a police officer. I always felt that if I was able to lay my head on my own pillow at the end of the day, it was a good day. There were days when my shift ended at the hospital, and I have known many good cops whose shifts ended at the morgue.

Chapter 6 Plug-In Points

- Every prayer is heard although not necessarily answered.
- Praying for others is an essential component of a spiritual practice.
- Your prayer list should include those people you are having trouble forgiving as well as those you don't know.
- Gratitude can be a major agent of change in your life. Feeling gratitude will raise your vibration.
- The theory the "Law of Attraction" states that you draw to you what you think about. Practicing gratitude may initiate a positive cycle by providing you with even more reasons to feel grateful.

CHAPTER 7

External Toxic Influences

J ust as your own negative or toxic thoughts and emotions can lower your frequency, so can external influences. Toxicity in this regard is defined as any influence that has a repeated negative effect on your health or sense of well-being or both.

The first place you should look for toxicity is within your home. Clutter is a vibrational influence—it does not serve to support you. Clutter in your external world reflects clutter in your internal world, your mind. Your first step toward making your home support a higher vibration is eliminating clutter. My policy is that if I haven't worn an article of clothing in the past year, then someone else can. I donate all clothes and shoes that fall into this category. My son is continuously growing; every new season prompts me to go through his clothes from the previous year, see what fits, and put the rest in a donation pile. I recommend starting with clothes and shoes first, before moving to other types of household clutter that often requires more thought. I do keep some things that I would call sentimental but not many.

When you have finished going through your entire house and ridding each area of clutter, you may find you have space for a spiritual altar in a corner or even a separate room. Your spiritual altar is a place for items that connect you to spirit and to your higher self. You can use this area as a refuge for meditation, writing in your journal, and peace.

After you've tackled the clutter issue, try to apply feng shui principles to your home. In simple terms, feng shui is an ancient Chinese approach to creating energy balance and harmony within your home. The basic concept is that placing material objects in a balanced and conscious manner will foster harmony. I subscribe to these principles and believe any home can have a positive or negative feel based on the manner in which the furniture and objects are placed. You can find much more information about feng shui by doing your own Internet search.

You can also cleanse the energy in your home by using white sage, an herb that can be found in your local organic or metaphysical store. Burning this herb within your home will cleanse all residual energies from your living space. This practice is also referred to as smudging. I believe that any new home should be cleansed with white sage. There will always be energies left behind by the previous occupants, and if they moved out due to bankruptcy, divorce, or death, the energies may not be positive. I also routinely smudge every time I clean my home.

Another issue that can foster a toxic environment within the home is discord between family members. An ongoing dispute between members of the household will cause an underlying tension, draining your energy and lowering your vibration. Consider opening lines of communication about the issue, and seek help from a family counselor if you think it necessary.

You should also examine the household cleaning products that you use in your home. Household chemicals can be both physically and therefore vibrationally toxic, so I strongly urge you to eliminate the toxic ones from your home. Consider that a small child in the crawling stage and your pet may spend much more time in contact with the residue from these products than you do. Instead of throwing out the cleaning products you already have, you can just phase in new ones. Look for safer products you can buy at the stores where you normally shop. Optimal cleaning products do not contain harsh chemicals or fumes and are safe for skin contact. Many cleaning products are eco-friendly and free of harsh chemicals. This isn't meant to be a product endorsement, but I switched to Mrs. Meyer's line of cleaning supplies several years ago. Its products are equally as powerful as the ones I had used before, and the prices are comparable to those of other cleaners.

One source of external toxity that you can eliminate without much effort is media. I am not advocating that you ignore current events. How can you pray for others in the world if you don't know what's happening? My suggestion for your media exposure is this: try getting your media only from Internet sources for a period of six months. If you like, you can choose to return to reading the newspaper or watching the nightly news on television after that. Why Internet only? Because you can pick and choose what news you want to expose yourself to.

Consider these news story headlines, each fictitious, and decide which you would want to read:

1. "Mother Kills Two Toddlers Before Setting the House on Fire"
2. "Angry Mob Overthrows Dictator"
3. "U.S. Car Manufacturer Recalls 2 Million Vehicles"
4. "Famous Actress Divorces Again"
5. "Body of Missing Teenager Found in Shallow Grave"
6. "Ongoing Gang Dispute in City Leaves 5 Shot and 3 Killed"

For the first story, I don't want to know any more than that headline (and part of me regrets seeing even that). It's upsetting and unfortunately frequent in our world today. There is nothing I can do, and there is nothing more I need to know about that event. However, I would definitely read the second story to learn more about what's happening in the world and to stay current. I would also want to know more about the vehicle recall in the third story, in case it affects me or a friend of family member. It's likely that I would avoid the fourth story, about the actress' divorce. I would skip the fifth story; the headline tells me how that story-line ended, I'm not a detective working the case, and I don't want to contaminate my mind with something so dark and negative. I would also skip the final story; unfortunately it's not news where I'm from but merely another event in a long line of events just like it.

Even though I'm not reading some of those news stories, I still care. I can pray for the families of those killed without knowing any more than the headline. That's my approach to media. I stopped watching Baltimore's television news when I retired; I don't need to stay current, and the stories are negative. In fact, the television news stories are oftentimes inaccurate. (I can say that as someone who has been at a crime scene and known the facts only to see another version on the 6 p.m. news.) My opinion of national news programs is only slightly better.

In addition to your home, toxicity can also be present in your work environment if you hate your work, aren't treated with respect at work, or both. No matter what you do to make a living, if you enjoy it and it's legal, then it's positive. My son and I were talking one day about how important it is that our garbage be removed. I pointed out to him that garbage removal is an important function and that no job is insignificant. He seemed to understand the simple concept that lingering garbage was bad. Whatever you do to pay the bills is important to someone, even if it's not your life's dream.

If your job meets your financial but not your emotional needs, try to focus on one or two positive aspects of it (and not the negative ones). Reframe the job as a temporary situation. Be grateful to have a job, and focus on that gratitude rather than what the job isn't doing for you. Look elsewhere for something that meets all of your needs, or resign yourself that it's your choice that you're staying. If you're not treated with respect in the job but the job pays the bills, you must consider the toll on your overall health and vibration before deciding to remain there. Respect is not optional; we must all give respect and demand it in return. You can't voluntarily stay and be bitter at the same time. Take responsibility for your choices.

Friends and relatives can also have a toxic effect on your life and therefore your health and vibration. I have two friends who no longer speak to their mothers because their mothers are toxic. It is a choice to remain engaged in a relationship that does not serve you positively. I am not saying it would be an easy decision to cut the cord with your mother or another close relative, but sometimes it must be done. If the relationship is abusive, it certainly requires examination. Except for children under the age of eighteen, all relationships in our lives are voluntary. We are not bound to anyone other than our children, and if our children become abusive adults that cord can be cut as well.

Years ago I noticed a pattern in my personal relationships that I've since made an effort to change: I did more giving than receiving. I had a history of relationships that were out of balance in this way. I also tended to attract negative, worrying people. These negative people would stop by my office or call me to get a little of my optimism before returning to their full time residence on "Misery Lane." Sometimes these folks were more than just miserable: they were energy vampires. When they left, I'd feel slightly depleted and they'd feel a bit better. I've done my best to eliminate these types of people from my life. No matter what you call them, they are toxic and your continued contact with them is optional.

Peaceful sanctuary.

Chapter 7 Plug-In Points

- External toxic influences will affect your health and lower your vibration.
- Clutter is toxic.
- Create a spiritual space within your home where you can find refuge for meditation, writing in your journal, and peace.
- Routinely cleanse the energy in your home with white sage.
- Chemical cleaning products can be toxic to you and your family.
- Media sources should be viewed in a limited fashion and with discretion.
- Your work environment affects your vibration either positively or negatively.
- All relationships with friends and even relatives are optional; if they take more than they add to your life, you must make a choice.

CHAPTER 8

The Language of Spirit

To receive messages from your spirit guides, you must first openly announce your intention to become a willing channel. Yes, a spirit guide can read your thoughts, but you must ask. You can simply say aloud, "I am open to receive messages from the highest possible source," prior to your meditation session.

Why do you need to specify a source for the messages? Imagine opening your front door and inviting anyone who wanted to come in to do so. That would be a problem, right? You don't want to be missing the family silverware after they leave. You must specify that you only want to speak to the highest possible source from the light. I don't want to scare you, but as a novice you are vulnerable to spirits from a darker place who may try to communicate with you. This happened to me a few times when I first began channeling until I learned to discern who was speaking to me.

My last assignment as a police officer was in the motorcycle unit. Motor officers are killed every year in vehicle crashes and intentional acts of violence due to their vulnerability. I remember the first time I went to the National Law Enforcement Officers Memorial in Washington, D.C., and saw how many boots and helmets were placed beneath motor officer names on the wall. Fellow officers leave behind artifacts and other mementos near their comrade's name to honor him or her.

I knew the motorcycle assignment was a dangerous job, but I had been on the SWAT team years earlier and had never felt as vulnerable in that position as I did on motorcycle patrol. My fear was not of dying in the line of duty—I don't fear death and never have. My biggest fear was of being paralyzed from a crash. One day while meditating, I heard a voice say, "You will be asked to make a sacrifice." I was then shown an image of a man I knew who had recently become paraplegic due to an accident. I was terrified. Would this be my fate too? The image and the message stayed with me for at least a full day.

Then I remembered a sentence I had read in the book *Open to Channel*, by Sanaya Roman and Duane Packer. (I highly recommend this book to anyone who wants to channel.) The authors said that you will always know you have been speaking with a spirit of the light when you feel good after the encounter. Feeling bad after the encounter is an indication you were speaking with a spirit not of the light. Their statement clicked, and I realized the dark side had fooled me.

Why does the dark side do that? Dark spirits feed on your worry and fear, which provide energy that empowers them. In addition, the worry and fear temporarily lowers your vibration. Remember this golden rule and you will be safe: disregard any information from spirit that does not leave you feeling good. You will never be told the date and manner of your death or anything similarly negative.

Why did spirit insist that I figure that out by myself? Because it is a lesson that must be learned to navigate in the spirit world. Just like our physical world, the spirit world contains good and bad and some in between. If you are ever afraid of a spiritual energy around you or even just uneasy, call for Archangel Michael and ask for his assistance. He is extremely powerful and will protect you.

After you have opened yourself up to receive messages from light spirits, you may receive the messages in various ways. If you hear the messages, as I do, you are considered *clairaudient*. If you receive the messages visually, you are considered *clairvoyant*. If you have an inner knowing, you are receiving messages in a *clairsentient* manner. I have received messages in all three formats but prefer to hear my messages. I believe we are each wired to receive in our own unique way or combination of ways.

Another way I have received information is *empathically*, feeling what it is like to be someone else. Usually this happens when I'm giving Reiki to other people, but occasionally it happens when I'm simply close enough physically that my energy field overlaps with someone else's. For example, one time I was posing for a picture with a coworker. When I placed my left hand (passive hand that receives energy) on her back (her heart chakra), I felt overwhelming sadness and grief. I don't know this woman well enough to understand the details of her feelings, but the experience was startling. Receiving empathic information is the quickest way to know how someone else is feeling.

Spirit knows how to reach you, and I believe we each receive in a way best suited for us. Like lots of people, I sometimes get a knowing feeling about situations or other people. It's a comfortable way to receive information—not too disruptive to our day-to-day lives. Spirit also likes to speak to me in images, which can convey an entire message. Sometimes I don't understand the image, and I say so. Usually if I'm unsuccessful in figuring it out, the spirit guide will clarify the message by giving me words to accompany the image.

For example, one day I was in a work meeting chaired by my boss at the time. She is a powerful woman whose behavior is known to be bullying and abusive, depending on her mood and the perceived infraction. I noticed she was wearing a beautiful cross necklace with embedded diamonds. I stopped to wonder what the symbol of Jesus meant to her and why she wore it. She did not appear, at least to me, to embody the philosophies of Christ in her outward life. Spirit showed me an image of M&T Bank Stadium full of fans during a Baltimore Ravens professional football game. The seats were filled with people wearing the home team's purple and black jersey. I understood right away: just because you're wearing the jersey doesn't mean you're in the game.

This is how spirit speaks to us. This example was tailored for me. If it had been meant for you, perhaps another image (or sports team) would have been shown to you. Spirit guides know your mind and what images will best deliver their message to you. If you don't understand the message, ask for clarity. There have been many times when I told the spirit guides I did not understand the image's meaning. They always follow up with additional information, doing whatever they can to ensure I understand.

Spirit also speaks through recurring messages or patterns. Last week, I was walking in my neighborhood and found a small baby rabbit on the sidewalk. His back legs did not work, and it appeared that his back might be broken. I took him home and cared for him, but he died within twenty-four hours.

The following week, I was again walking through my neighborhood. This time I found a baby blue jay on the sidewalk. It had its flight feathers but seemingly couldn't fly. I picked it up and placed it in a tree, because a cat had been stalking it. I continued my walk and reflected on the odd coincidence of finding two creatures in a similar state within a week's time.

I decided that this had been no coincidence at all and that there was a message in it for me. After thinking for a few minutes, I said to spirit, "What do you want me to see here?"

Spirit said, "Both animals are incapable of movement."

"Meaning what?" I asked.

"You need to move on," was the reply.

I knew what spirit was referring to: I had an emotional attachment that was not good for me, yet I could not seem to leave it behind. I said, "I think I've had some momentum there."

Spirit showed me a car stuck in a rut, spinning its wheels.

I got the idea: It may seem like you're moving even when you're not going anywhere. So I said, "I understand the meaning now. I need your help with this. I need guidance on how to let this go."

"Close this chapter so another one can begin," was the response.

Another example of a repeated pattern or a reoccurring message:

I was unloading the dishwasher yesterday and the top shelf was stuck. I kept pulling forward and it wouldn't budge. I moved a glass, no movement. I moved something else and it was still stubbornly stuck. I peered into the dishwasher and saw what was holding it back and moved it. Finally, I was able to move the shelf out and unload it. A few minutes later, I went into my office looking for tape. I opened the drawer of my desk and it was stuck. I played around with a few objects and got it to open. I then got in my car and turned on the Dr. Laura show. She is a psychologist on Sirius XM radio, if you've not heard of her. A woman called in for advice and Dr. Laura told her she was stuck.

Wait just a minute here! How many times do I need the message "STUCK" before I notice that spirit is telling me something? This is how spirit speaks in repeated messages. If you ever find yourself in this situation, disregard the inclination to think it's a coincidence and look for the meaning. Nothing is random and there are no coincidences. If you keep that in mind, you will always look beyond the obvious. If you don't understand the message, ask for more information.

Chapter 8 Plug-in Points

- When attempting to connect with spirit, you must state that you wish to speak only with the light.
- You will always know when the light has contacted you, because the encounter will leave you feeling good.
- People receive messages in a variety of ways: audibly, visually, by an inner knowing, empathically, and combinations of these.
- Images are the preferred language of spirit.
- Recurring messages should be examined for deeper meaning.

CHAPTER 9

Physical versus Extrasensory Perception

Messages from spirit come to you through your third eye and crown chakras in a manner termed extrasensory perception. It's called extrasensory, because the information cannot be perceived through the five established physical senses: sight, hearing, taste, touch, and smell.

Your senses of sight, touch, and hearing are dominant over your senses of taste and smell. This hierarchy has evolved to protect us, because threats to our physical security are not usually perceived through taste and smell. (Note that this is not a strict rule: there are exceptions such as smelling smoke from a fire and tasting spoiled potato salad at a cookout.)

Imagine you and your spouse are walking into a friend's new home for the first time. You're taking it all in—the decor, the sound of voices echoing against the high ceiling, and the feeling of her dog jumping on your leg again and again. Your spouse says to you, "Wow, dinner smells delicious." When you isolate your sense of smell and inhale deeply, you realize that something does smell wonderful. This is an example of how you have to shut down the dominant senses to perceive a more subtle sense.

Another example could be a captivating conversation while eating dinner with a new companion. When you finish eating and realize you barely tasted your meal, your dominant senses have kept you engaged in the conversation rather than with your dinner.

Your sixth sense, your extrasensory perception, is even less noticeable than your senses of smell and taste. It must be acknowledged, and your physical senses must be isolated and shut down for a moment. Sometimes I receive information from spirit by seeing with my physical sight and hearing with my ears, but usually information comes to me through this much more subtle avenue.

When I receive messages from spirit through extrasensory perception, I typically feel a buzzing vibration around my eyes. Sometimes this sensation encompasses my entire head. My mentor, Dekiva, calls it my "marker." She tells me her back feels like it's buzzing when she receives messages. I believe each of us feels a different sensation when we receive spirit's energy and that this sensation is based on our energy signature and the level of the spirit with whom we're in contact. The buzzing around my eyes instantly makes me aware that a higher level of spirit is with me.

One time I was at a dimly lit restaurant in Virginia with JoAnn, one of my best friends. We had just ordered an appetizer and drinks. JoAnn was seated to my right, and the chair directly across from me was ostensibly vacant yet a mist was floating in it. I looked at the mist, looked away, and looked again at the chair. As JoAnn continued talking, I began searching for a plausible explanation. Finally, I stopped her and said, "Do you see a mist in that chair?" She looked at the chair and said she saw nothing. At first I was a little confused. Finally, I focused on my third eye, isolating it over my physical senses, to see if I could get more information. What did I see with my mind's eye?

Sitting in the chair was a Southern gentleman wearing a Confederate dress uniform. He seemed a little smug. When I noticed him, he said, "You two are the most interesting people in here. Do you mind if I sit with you?" I told him I didn't mind, and he said nothing further but remained with us for a while even after we left the restaurant. This is an example of how I receive information from my third eye, my extrasensory perception. You may work in a different manner.

The next time you're watching television and a commercial for a pharmaceutical product comes on, consider the following:

The commercial will frequently show a person who is now capable of having a much more active or enjoyable life due to the amazing, magical drug being marketed. The beginning of the commercial is visually stimulating and underlines how the person's life has improved. As a viewer, you may barely hear the narrator's voice-over. Then, the screen becomes even more vivid, and the narrator recites a long list of the drug's potential side effects. The colors and idyllic images shown during this disclaimer are so compelling that even a discerning viewer may be distracted momentarily. Then you'll realize that the advertiser is relying on your dominant sense (sight) to override the negative aspects of the drug so that the commercial can leave you with a positive impression.

Typically, the same drug commercial will be shown multiple times during a one-hour television show. The first time you watch the commercial, mute the television's volume, focus only on the visuals, and summarize the experience in three words. For example, I might say, "Empowering, fun, beautiful." When the commercial is replayed, close your eyes and only listen to the narrative. You will be shocked at the difference in your experience.

Chapter 9 Plug-in Points

- Your senses of sight, hearing, and touch are dominant over your senses of taste and smell.
- Extrasensory perception is more subtle than any of your physical senses.
- You must quiet your physical sensory perceptions to receive extrasensory messages.
- When spirit is trying to connect with you, you will feel a physical sensation somewhere in your body (a "marker") that is unique to you, your energy field, and the energy of the spirit with whom you are connecting. Your marker will alert you that a spirit is trying to connect with you.

CHAPTER 10

Being Persistent

Last weekend I went for a hike on the Appalachian Trail. This was a new spot for me, and the hike began with a two-mile trek uphill on very rocky terrain. I'm in decent shape for someone my age, but I was panting and sweating profusely during the climb. Near the top, I came across a woman sitting on a rock. I asked her if the top was very much farther, and she said she didn't know. She had told her friends to continue without her and that she would reconnect with them on their way back down. I thanked her and kept walking.

Within five minutes, the trail leveled out significantly and became much easier. I heard my guides say, "She stopped right before it got easier." The words lingered in my mind. I knew their message had a broader application. Spirit asked me to relate this to you: You never know when your breakthrough is coming, so don't stop trying. Most likely it will not happen right away. Continue to try anyway. It's important and your spirit guides want to reach you, so keep trying new techniques to make contact. Your breakthrough will be the most amazing moment of your life and well worth the effort.

I recommend you seek out a spiritual advisor or mentor who will help you as questions come up during your journey. My only warning is that there are just as many disreputable people who claim to be psychic as there are genuine ones with ability and good intentions. Ask spirit to guide you to a mentor, to make your paths cross. My first mentor had a card at my acupuncturist's office on a table of advertisements from holistic practitioners. I asked my acupuncturist if the mentor was any good and received a positive recommendation. Make sure whoever you choose is recommended by someone whose opinion you trust. This will be a vulnerable time in your development—please place your trust in someone safe and reliable.

After clearing the clutter (refer back to chapter 1), hopefully you've been able to create a spiritual area or room within your home. My sacred space contains a few religious items, incense, candles, spiritual books, sea shells, rocks from my hikes, and other things that either relax me or remind me why I'm there. My meditation room is not used for much else, so the energy in there is clean and refreshing—perfect for channeling.

If you cannot set aside some space that is solely yours, find a suitable area where you won't be interrupted. Smudge the area prior to each meditation, and ask that the area be cleansed of all residual energies that are not conducive to reception. Place a few special items in front of you or nearby for the desired effect. Let your family know that you need some time to yourself and shouldn't be interrupted. Make sure phones are not going to disturb you and that your pets are out of the room. The smallest distraction could take you off course.

You can sit either in a chair or on the floor. It isn't advisable to lie on a bed, because you might fall asleep there. Find a position that is comfortable but not conducive to sleep. I sit on the floor with my feet outstretched and lean on something for back support. You can start in the traditional lotus position (a cross-legged sitting position used in yoga in which each foot is on the thigh of the opposite leg) if you're that flexible, but it's really not necessary. If a position is at all uncomfortable for you, it's not advisable. Keep making adjustments until you find the right position. I have found that something as seemingly insignificant as hand position can make a difference. During one session, I changed my hand position from palms up and resting on my knees to one hand cupped inside the other and the messages started coming in. I don't fully understand the reason for this, but I believe it's related to the flow of energy in the body. Experiment with positioning and consider it an important aspect of your meditation and channeling process.

Meditate for at least ten minutes prior to beginning your channeling session. As discussed earlier, mediation is merely wiping your mind free of thought. It can be done anywhere and in any pose that you find comfortable. The only caveat is that you must be in an environment that is free of distraction.

At the end of your meditation, begin thinking of a person or animal for whom you feel nothing but uncomplicated love. There is nothing negative about this relationship. Think about this person or pet, how much you love him or her, how wonderful he or she is, how you're so lucky to have him or her in your life, and so forth. Sitting in this atmosphere of unconditional love will put you in the proper vibration of spirit. Think about this love for at least five minutes before moving to the next step. If you've had a bad day or feel "off," you may need to stay with this thought longer.

Next, state that you want to receive messages from the highest level of spirit (recall this from chapter 8). I then say the Lord's Prayer, because I feel that its positive message elevates my vibration. I know this appears to be in conflict with my earlier comments that reading from a book is not a spiritual practice. The difference is that I am not reading this prayer: it is in my heart and mind.

In the following chapter, I will provide you with some of the imaging exercises I used when I first began to reach for spirit. Because my energy tends to be grounded, the exercises that worked for me are focused on raising my vibration to a level that makes it possible to receive spirit. If you have a strong crown, you will probably not benefit from the same exercises that worked for me. The exercises are marked as either "best for people with grounded energy" (most helpful if your energy is stronger below the waist) and "best for people with crown chakra energy" (most helpful if your energy field is stronger above the waist). Different energy fields require different visualization exercises, so I have included a variety. Begin by trying them all to determine which work best for you.

Obviously you cannot achieve reception and read at the same time. I recommend that you either memorize the exercise and then re-create the process, or read this section into a recorder (your mobile phone probably has one). You will find listening to your own voice distracting, so you may need to hear the sessions a few times to get past that obstacle.

Keep going until you get there.

The Receptivity Project

Chapter 10 Plug-in Points

- Be persistent in your efforts to channel.
- Seek a spiritual mentor who is recommended by someone you trust.
- Use a sacred space for meditation and channeling.
- Begin your channeling sessions by meditating.
- Infuse your energy field with love by thinking of love.
- Make clear that you only want to receive messages from the light, and ask for protection.
- The visualization exercises provided in the following chapter vary; find one that works for you and adapt it as needed.

CHAPTER 11

Visualization Exercises

Exercise One
(Best for People with Grounded Energy)

Begin this exercise by thinking of a person or pet you love without reservation. You should feel nothing but pure love for them. Focus on that
image and emotion for at least five minutes, thinking and feeling complete,
pure love. Focus all of your thoughts and emotions on this subject. Beginning your
visualization exercises with this love vibration will enhance your efforts to channel.

Then, recite the following:
I am safe and loved by the energies I am about to connect with. I am asking to communicate only with the highest level of spirit. I ask that Archangel
Michael protect me from the darkness during this time and always. I am about
to meet my spirit guides.

Then, imagine yourself in the following situation:
You're sitting in a room in which an elevator has appeared. You've never seen
this elevator before. There is only one button on the outside of the elevator, and
you press it. The elevator opens, and you enter it, knowing that you are safe and
loved. You are about to meet your spirit guides, and you know it will be an amazing experience. Your guides have so much to tell you, so much love for you.

After entering the elevator, you turn to face the door. You see buttons to
the right of the door. They are labeled in words and various colors. You press the

button at the top of the list, labeled "My Guides." The doors close, and the elevator begins to climb.

A pleasant voice alerts you as the elevator stops at each floor on its way to the top floor, the twelfth. When the door opens at each floor, visualize yourself leaving a metaphorical package there, then the door closing again:

First floor: Leave all stress on this floor.

Second floor: Leave all physical pain on this floor.

Third floor: Leave all emotional pain on this floor.

Fourth floor: Leave all judgment on this floor.

Fifth floor: Leave all resentment on this floor.

Sixth floor: Leave ego on this floor.

Seventh floor: Leave your human personality on this floor.

Eighth floor: Release any expectations you have about how the channeling process will develop on this floor.

Ninth floor: Leave your physical body on this floor.

Tenth floor: Leave the pain of all your past lives on this floor.

Eleventh floor: Cleanse your mind and leave scattered thoughts on this floor.

Twelfth floor: This floor is where you will meet your guides. Exit the elevator and maintain an open mind and clear heart. As you exit the elevator, the doors close behind you.

You are now standing in a room full of white light streaming in from many windows. The white light surrounds you, and you feel it enter your soul. You have left so much behind during the elevator ride, so many things that were weighing you down. You feel weightless, light as a feather. You feel safe and loved, knowing that you are in a place of truth, light, and love. Now you ask that your guides introduce themselves.

Clear your mind and wait. You must keep your mind completely empty so the guides can send you a message. Consider anything that seems unfamiliar or odd to you during this time to be a possible message. If you are shown an image, reflect on it and try to discern its meaning. If you don't understand, say so. If you're unsure, ask for clarification. The guides want you to understand, so your questions will not offend them.

Pay attention to the energy around you. If you receive energy much higher than your own, you may begin to breathe heavily and ultimately go into a trance. If the energy level you receive is more consistent with your own, you likely won't go into a trance. It all depends on the energy of the spirit coming through.

You may feel a buzzing about your head or elsewhere within your body. If you hear the phrase "go higher," "reach for us," or anything similar, you are on the right track! You are close to receiving spirit guides. At that point they have come as low as they can and they need you to go up more to meet them. Continue with the visualization, creating another image that takes you upward. You may want to ride in an air balloon or on an escalator. If you liked the elevator concept from earlier, get back into the elevator, see that there are now additional buttons, and ride up a few more floors. Adjust the exercise as necessary to reach your spirit guides.

Exercise Two
(Best for People with Grounded Energy)

Begin this exercise by thinking of a person or pet you love without reservation. You should feel nothing but pure love for them. Focus on that image and emotion for at least five minutes, thinking and feeling complete, pure love. Focus all of your thoughts and emotions on this subject. Beginning your visualization exercises with this love vibration will enhance your efforts to channel.

Then, recite the following:
I am safe and loved the by energies I am about to connect with. I am asking to communicate only with the highest level of spirit. I ask that Archangel Michael protect me from the darkness during this time and always. I am about to meet my spirit guides.

Then, imagine yourself in the following situation:
You are standing in front of a huge Mayan pyramid. The top of the pyramid seems very far away. You are carrying a large, heavy sack on your back. You don't think you can climb to the top while carrying this heavy load. But as soon as you have this thought, an angel dressed entirely in white appears. She says she will assist you on the journey. She asks you to begin climbing the pyramid with her. You tell her you're not sure you can do it. She asks you to give her something to hold so that your burden will be lightened. You reach into the sack and hand her a

box labeled "judgment." She takes this box from you and it tosses it aside. She says, "You are relieved of this burden."

You climb with her for a minute or so until you are out of breath, and then you tell her you need her help again. She asks for another parcel from the sack, so you reach into the sack and take out a box labeled "regrets." She takes the box and tosses it down to the ground. She says, "You are relieved of this burden."

You continue to climb together until you ask her for help again. At her urging, you reach into the sack and pull out three different boxes: they are labeled "self-loathing," "resentment," and "expectations." She takes the three boxes, and they disappear from her hands before your eyes. She says, "They are no more. We have reached a level too high for them to exist."

You continue to climb the stairs of the enormous pyramid. You stop after another minute. You don't need to talk now—you just know what to do. You reach into the sack, pull out a box labeled "pain," and hand the box to her. It's gone. The sack is very light now, but you want it to be empty when you reach the top. The sack and its contents no longer serve you on your journey. You reach into the sack and hand her two more boxes: "ego" and "need for control." She takes these burdens from you.

The sack is now empty. You have never felt this light. You feel that if you were to jump off the pyramid you would fly. The angel smiles at you—she knows your every thought. You continue to climb, and it is no longer difficult. You are close to the top of the pyramid now, and you feel the tingling of the elevation around your head and body. The view is so beautiful. Everything and everyone in your life seems quite small from here—your house looks like you could hold it in your hand.

You've reached the top of the pyramid. You will wait here for your messages from spirit. You are an open channel and at the top of your range of vibration. You are now capable of receiving messages from your guides.

Exercise Three
(Best for People with Grounded Energy)

Begin this exercise by thinking of a person or pet you love without reservation. You should feel nothing but pure love for them. Focus on that image and emotion for at least five minutes, thinking and feeling complete, pure love. Focus all of your thoughts and emotions on this subject. Beginning your visualization exercises with this love vibration will enhance your efforts to channel.

Then, recite the following:
I am safe and loved by the energies I am about to connect with. I am asking to communicate only with the highest level of spirit. I ask that Archangel Michael protect me from the darkness during this time and always. I am about to meet my spirit guides.

Then, imagine yourself in the following situation:
You are standing in a beautiful field full of fresh flowers and butterflies on a warm, sunny day. You see a hot air balloon staked to the ground in the middle of the field. You walk over to the hot air balloon and see that Jesus is in it, smiling at you. He gestures with His hand for you to enter the balloon basket. You do so. Standing next to Him, you realize that His energy is the most beautiful energy you have ever felt in your life. He radiates pure love.

Archangel Michael appears and, with his sword, cuts the ropes that tie down the balloon. You ascend. After a few seconds, only about twenty feet from the ground, the balloon appears to stall. You look at the basket's floor and see several boxes that appear to be weighing down the balloon. They are each labeled. You look at Jesus, and He merely nods at you. You pick up a box labeled "ego." Jesus nods again, and you throw the box out of the balloon basket. You know there is more weighing down the balloon. You pick up another box, this one labeled "judgment." You toss it out of the basket as well. Relieved of the extra weight of these two boxes, the balloon rises, then stalls again.

You pick up another box, this one quite heavy. It is labeled "pain." You toss this box out of the basket. The balloon instantly rises further.

Jesus is guiding the balloon to a safe place. He is in control now and always. He loves you and is taking you to a better place. You know you can lighten the burden even more, so you quickly pick up the remaining boxes and toss "jealousy," "resentment," "lack of forgiveness," and "hatred" out of the basket. The balloon soars. You know you are on a marvelous journey and safe with the beautiful and powerful energy of Jesus Christ. He will take you where you need to go and show you what you need to know. You are now open to all possibilities.

Exercise Four
(Best for People with Crown Chakra Energy)

Begin this exercise by thinking of a person or pet you love without reservation. You should feel nothing but pure love for them. Focus on that image and emotion for at least five minutes, thinking and feeling complete, pure love. Focus all of your thoughts and emotions on this subject. Beginning your visualization exercises with this love vibration will enhance your efforts to channel.

Then, recite the following:

I am safe and loved by the energies I am about to connect with. I am asking to communicate only with the highest level of spirit. I ask that Archangel Michael protect me from the darkness during this time and always. I am about to meet my spirit guides.

Then, imagine yourself in the following situation:

You are hiking in the woods when you come across an opening in a rock formation. You realize you've found a cave. You'd like to explore the cave, but it's dark and you have no flashlight. You take a few steps inside and see a man, wearing all white, with long, white hair and a long, white beard. He hands you a torch to light the way. You begin to navigate through this huge cavernous area and, as you walk, you realize the man is following you. His energy feels completely safe, and you intuitively know he is looking after you on your journey into the unknown. He is your guide.

As you walk, the path begins to slope downward. The cave is damp and dark, and you can feel the energy of the earth all around you as you descend. You become concerned that you will not be able to find your way back out and wonder how you can mark your way. Your silent guide points to your pants pocket, and you realize it feels rather bulky. You reach in and find a rock that you can place on the ground as a marker. Oddly enough, the rock is labeled "old wounds."

You continue on your journey. When you feel the need to lay down another marker for your return to the surface, you fish another rock out of your pocket. It is marked "worry." You place it on the ground and continue walking. You lay down another rock every hundred feet or so as you continue on your journey downward toward something that feels absolutely wonderful. These rocks are labeled "resentment," "envy," "control," and "judgment." You continue walking and realize that without these rocks in your pocket, you feel much lighter and at ease. The path is easier without the weight of these burdens.

You hear something behind you and realize your guide is still with you. He smiles at you and nods; you intuitively know you are about to meet more guides. You have traveled very far beneath the earth's surface, and you feel the buzzing and power of the planet's energy. You pull the grounded energy in through your root chakra. You are now calm and balanced.

You reach a wall of rocks and realize that what you seek is just behind it. You and your guide begin removing the rocks, one by one. You enjoy the feel of these rocks in your hands as you work to remove the obstacle between you and your guides. The wall is getting shorter as you work. You are completely safe and ready to receive the messages your guides are eager to share with you. When you have finished tearing down the wall, you step into their realm. Envision a blank chalkboard in your mind. When you achieve this blankness, you have reached spirit's realm and are capable of receiving messages from your guides.

Special considerations related to the crown chakra: Because people whose energy is focused in the crown chakra have the most difficulty clearing their minds, I suggest the concept of the blank chalkboard so that your mind has something to attach to during this phase. Spirit says the human mind is like a drowning swimmer desperately trying to grab onto something.

Spirit has asked me to illustrate this point to you by using the following example:

BREAK

Typically, the word *break* is linked to another word to give it meaning. It has meaning as a stand-alone word, but it has more depth of meaning when linked to another word or a series of words. Don't understand?

Being given a lucky break, is a good thing. Your spouse calling to say he or she wants a break from your relationship is not so good. Your doctor using the word break in a sentence is also not good. A break in the action could be good or bad, depending on the type of action. A car breakdown is never a good thing, a nervous breakdown is even worse. A break can be a vacation or a painful injury. These illustrations are intended to show how our mind works and how we attach meaning to everything. The word break begs for context in our minds. The mind has a similar stickiness factor that causes it to struggle when unattached and free from thought. Like a drowning swimmer, it feels out of control and in need of certainty. Allow your mind to float without struggling.

You may feel a buzzing about your crown or you may not. If the energy in your crown is significant, you may not discern a difference during your channeling session. Be aware of any buzzing about your body and be open to energy around you that is not part of your own energy field. Just like a telephone conversation, you can't speak and hear what someone is saying at the same time. You can't think and receive messages from your guides at the same time. They require a break in your thoughts, a blank space, to reach you. When it comes to channeling, crown energy is both a blessing and a challenge. You must harness the energy of your mind in order to allow spirit to break through.

Alternatives to Try

I've provided these visualization exercises so you have a few to choose from. Perhaps one exercise resonates with you more than the others do. You can change the types of burdens that are released to fit what you've been working on in your life. If your boss is your main source of stress, you may want to label a box with his or her name or picture.

If the imagery of these exercises doesn't resonate with you, create your own. The purpose of such an exercise is to adjust your vibration range to be accessible to spirit. These are generic examples with many possible variations. Some people may respond best to climbing imagery, while others may find descending imagery more effective. I have always used a climbing visualization, because it raises my vibration. If you need to do the opposite, then design a visualization that grounds you.

Besides visualization, another option you may want to consider is automatic writing. After a brief meditation to clear your mind and open up to receive spirit's messages, sit with pen and paper. Allow spirit to control your hand, and begin writing. Do not edit or even acknowledge what is being written. Keep going until you feel that the flow has stopped. This is similar but different from what I do when I write down messages that I receive while in a trance. From what I understand about automatic writing, the writer does not know what has been written until he or she has finished and read it. Some people have great success with this.

The white lotus flower rises to the surface from the mud below.
It is a Buddhist symbol that represents mental purity.

Chapter 11 Plug-in Points

- Find one visualization exercise that resonates best with you. The exercise could be one of the generic ones provided here, an adaptation of one of these, or a new variation you design.
- Edit the imagery of the exercise to match your emotional needs.
- Automatic writing is another option you may want to explore for receiving messages from spirit.

CHAPTER 12

Fusing Auras

I f you've tried visualization exercises and, after a period of effort and dedication, you're still unsuccessful, you may benefit from having a meditation partner. The trick is that you will need to find someone who has the opposite energetic composition to your own. I have lower-chakra strength, therefore I partner best with someone who has a strong crown chakra. I would recommend that you and your partner take turns, attempting to channel spirit for one of you at a time.

When I channel with a crown–chakra-focused person, I want to "hold the ground" for him or her. Use imagery to keep you on the ground while he or she meditates. You can envision a hot air balloon tethered to the ground or something similar. I envision myself holding a kite tied down to the earth. The resulting energy field will slow down your partner's crown energy, therefore slowing the activity within his or her mind.

Sit back-to-back with your meditation partner. If you are different heights, use pillows to align your chakras to the extent possible. You are attempting to fuse your energy fields, with the synergy of the union enhancing both; the total will be greater than the sum of the parts. The two partners must decide in advance which one will attempt to connect with spirit first, so that the other person can maintain his or her frequency. One of you may choose to assist the other by reading the appropriate visualization exercise aloud. Work together. Ask for spirit to show you how to make your partnership work for the greatest good.

When it's time for the partners to switch roles, the crown-oriented person can imagine a kite flying through the air, themselves flying, or anything else that keeps them high enough to support and elevate the energy for both people. You are attempting to maintain your own energy frequency and alter the other person's, which sometimes requires conscious effort. If you are of a very high vibration, you may only need to sit there and allow your partner access to your energy.

Recently, I gave a Reiki demonstration to a small class. The woman I as using for the demonstration was lying on a massage table. She was so strong in her crown chakra that I began slipping away into the semiconscious trance that precedes channeling for me. I wasn't even touching her; I was about two feet away from her. I stepped away until I no longer felt her energy. I recognized that if I didn't consciously hold the ground, she was strong enough to raise me out of consciousness. I envisioned being anchored and then stepped back, more prepared to deal with the situation. You must be conscious in your efforts to maintain your energy for your partner's benefit. Working with a partner can assist you in in your efforts to channel. A meditation group or channeling class may also provide you with enough balancing-chakra energy to get you into the range required for you to channel.

Spirit wants me to explain that the road to channeling is like the neural pathways in your brain. The more you receive spirit's energy in this manner, the more the connections will be established, and the easier reception will become. The process is similar to the transformation of an unpaved path to a well-worn road: as more cars drive on it, it becomes more entrenched.

It may take you several attempts, months, or even years before you see results. If you feel you are stuck, review the food tips in chapter 4, make sure you're rested, and look for mental and emotional ways to improve your receptivity. Get help from someone experienced, or work with a mentor if necessary. Remember, don't stop right before it gets easier.

If you find you are a trance channeler, someone who is not fully conscious while receiving messages from spirit, don't be alarmed. I can receive in a fully conscious state or slip away to the point that I have trouble coming back, depending on the frequency of the energy I am channeling. When I am very far under, I simply ask spirit to step back so I can return to consciousness. It took me quite some time to realize that I can come out of a trance this way. Remember that you are always in control: light spirit will never put you in a position to be afraid or feel anything negative. On a logistical note, I usually keep pen and paper handy during my sessions, because I know that sometimes when I return to a conscious state I don't fully remember what has transpired. Remember, you should always feel good after channeling. My spirit guides told me early on, "We know your limitations and will work within them." This is true for you as well. If you want to want to "turn it off" once you begin to receive more consistently, you can. Simply tell spirit you need a break, and ask your guides to leave you alone for a day, a week, or whatever period of time you need. In fact, when I first opened the door to spirit, I found the chatter in my head a bit distracting. On a few occasions, I asked for twenty-four hours of quiet. You will probably find, as I did, that you will miss spirit's voice after you've become accustomed to it. It is your choice whether to receive, however, and your spirit guides will respect your request.

Ask for what you need. My spirit guides have told me that there is a special place for those who operate in the mode of receiver. They say there are so few of us who are willing. Your spirit guides will do whatever they can do, within the laws under which they operate, to assist you.

Be aware that the reverse is also true. Because there are so few who receive, you may be asked to assist spirit with requests. Don't be alarmed; they won't ask anything you can't handle. They may ask you to stop and interact with a homeless person or perform some other task. I can't say it won't be anything difficult, because I don't know your objectives or your capabilities. I can only say that it is your personal choice whether to assist them and it's rewarding to know you have helped someone.

Chapter 12 Plug-in Points

- Find a meditation partner whose energy field is opposite to your own.
- Fuse your auras by sitting back-to-back and aligning your chakras before meditating; this should allow both of your energy fields to balance more quickly.
- The more often you channel spirit, the easier it becomes.
- Trance channeling is not unusual, so do not be deterred if this is your manner of receiving spirit. If you trance channel, make sure you write during the session, because afterward you may not remember what happened. To come out of the trance, ask spirit to step back so you can return to consciousness.
- Ask spirit for what you need.

CHAPTER 13

Detaching from Expectations

"I am energy, not an elephant." ~ Ganesh
as channeled by Leslie N. Bank

was raised in a Jewish family and was taught Judaism in Sunday school until my Bat Mitzvah at age thirteen. But organized religion never resonated with me.

Because of my Jewish upbringing, I was surprised to find that my spirit guides are from other schools of thought. One of my first guides was Ganesh, a Hindu deity with an elephant head. Other guides who have spoken to me are from Christianity, Catholicism in particular. I was not expecting to have contact with these energies, because I was confident they didn't even exist.

I'm relating this to you to suggest that you abandon all expectations about the identity and nature of the guides with whom you may have contact. You will be addressed by guides who have something to say to you. They may or may not be the guides you are expecting. You may be a staunch Catholic hoping that the Blessed Mother has a message for you. The Buddha may show up instead. We don't need to have a previous attachment to the messenger. Your guide may be an energy you have never heard of (admittedly, I had to search the Internet for information about Ganesh). Trust that you cannot possibly know what is best for you in this area. Spirit has messages for your growth and development. Thank them for all that they choose to impart to you

Some people who channel and have spoken publicly about their channeling experiences identify only one energy that they speak with. The energy may have a name for itself or it may not. It may be a collective energy or a singular one. This one-energy phenomenon has not been my experience, however. I do not dismiss those people's experiences, but rather I want you to know that there a variety of experiences out there. Yours will be unique to you and your needs.

Chapter 13 Plug-in Points

- Release any expectations about the identity of your spirit guides.
- You may channel one energy, a variety of energies, or one collective energy.
- Each channeler's experience is unique.

CHAPTER 14

Past Lives

Most people open to their spiritual nature acknowledge that they have had many past lives. I want you to consider that there may be information embedded in your past lives that has value to you in your present life. In those past lives, as in your present life, you had objectives and agreements with others. Some of those objectives were met and some of those agreements were honored. Some were not. The unfulfilled objectives and contracts from those past lives may have followed you into this one. This is called your karma. Karma is a little different from the expression "What goes around, comes around," which is largely based on a concept of punishment and reward.

If I save your life, you may decide in our next lives to assist me with something. If you had a tumultuous relationship in a past life, that energy may carry into this life and your present-day relationship with that person's current incarnation. If you accept the principle of karma, you accept that we do not have a clean slate when we enter an incarnation. We each have an important mission here—to propel our soul's evolution.

Obviously, we aren't all going to cure cancer, travel to the moon, or do something significant on a global level. But if, for example, you give up your child for adoption, you have fulfilled a contract and thus an objective. It might not be a global one, but it is life-changing for all involved.

When spirit speaks to me, it almost always conveys messages that are lessons of the heart. Spirit has shown me many times that love is all we are supposed to be doing here and love connections are what are most important. Although I know that's an objective for me, I still struggle to share some parts of myself with others.

My hypnotherapist friend assisted me with a past-life regression. We began by asking spirit to show me which past life was having the most effect on my present life. I knew as soon as the session began that I was going back to a past life that I had seen in a previous regression. With dread, I relived this terrible past life that I have now been shown twice. I was a man in what appeared to be seventeenth-century colonial America. I had a wife and two daughters. I was a silversmith by trade, and we lived in a modest home.

One day when I came home from work, my wife told me that one of our daughters had "taken sick" and was in bed. I went to my daughter's side and found her burning up with fever, semiconscious. I asked my wife about the illness, but she appeared to be in complete denial about the illness's severity. I rushed back into town to find the doctor.

The doctor accompanied me to our home and assessed my daughter's condition. He told me her fever would break by morning and instructed me to apply cold compresses to her head and body. He also gave me a liquid to rub on her skin. I stayed with her all night, following the doctor's instructions. She appeared very, very sick, and I was scared I would lose her.

I woke up the next morning, still by her side (I must have dozed off for a little bit). She was gone. She had passed while I was sleeping; she had not been gone long. I had the unfortunate task of telling my wife and other daughter.

In the days, weeks, months, and years that followed, my life was never the same. My wife and I were never able to recapture the closeness we had once had. My surviving daughter brought me some comfort, yet her presence also reminded me of what was lost. We never spoke of our grief as a family. As a man, I was not expected to express my grief outwardly. By the time my wife passed, she and I had nothing more than a living arrangement, no longer a real marriage. My surviving daughter was quite good to me in my old age. She and her husband took care of me and provided me with several grandchildren.

In that life, I was never able to get past the feeling that even though I did everything that was expected of me—I provided for my family by working daily, worshipped the "right way," and had healthy and clean habits—I was punished. Happiness was shown to me, then taken from me in the blink of an eye. I died a bitter man. My heart had closed after my daughter's death.

In my last moments of that life, I was surrounded by family. But I was ready to leave. I had been dead inside since the girl died; I was a shell of a human being. When someone came to help me cross over, I slipped away gladly.

During the hypnotherapy session, my friend asked, "What did you take away from that experience (lifetime)?" My reply was, "Attachments are painful."

I have carried this into my present life. Knowing that doesn't make it easier for me to make and sustain attachments, but it does help to know my goals. You can't fire at a target that you can't see. Look into the past to learn more about what you are supposed to be improving in the present. Your past lives contain important lessons for you.

A note of caution: As with Reiki and psychic practitioners, you should only see a hypnotherapist recommended by someone you know. You are vulnerable in that state, so the environment must be safe.

Chapter 14 Plug-in Points

- You have had many past lives.
- Your purpose in your present life can be found in the stories from your past lives.
- Troubled relationships in your present life can sometimes be explained by conflicts that occurred in a past life.
- Hypnotherapy is an excellent tool for connecting with your past lives to determine which are most relevant to this life and why.

CHAPTER 15

How Your Life Fits
Your Objectives

t helps to think about your life's purpose using the analogy of taking college courses toward a degree. You begin school by declaring your major, then you develop a course schedule that includes the required courses and some elective courses.

Before you incarnated into the physical form that is reading these pages, you were energy that we call the soul. At that time, you had access to all of your past lives—and all of your successes and failures in them—on a spiritual level. Spirit does not like the word failure and would prefer that I instead call these non-successes "deficiencies." There are issues that you handled well in the past and issues you have come into form again and again to try to handle better. Your soul was tasked with creating the life that will help you meet those life goals. Your soul knows what hasn't worked in the past, so it has written your program differently this time—perhaps building in some backup plans.

Consider a man born with two legs that do not work. He spent his entire life cursing God for his "worthless legs." He lived with a heart full of resentment and anger that he was cheated out of living a life like everyone else's. He was unable to overcome this physical and mental disability. He was never able to reconcile his mind to his body and therefore his life. He only saw his limitations, so he was never able to realize his potential. He died a bitter, lonely man. When his soul left his body and returned home to spirit, he realized that it was he who had asked for two legs that did not work. Consistent with his life objective of learning gratitude in the face of adversity, he had incorporated the disability into his program before incarnating. It was not God's choice but his own. He was saddened to realize he must enter his next life in a similar condition to finally achieve the objective.

What exists in your life that you may, in fact, have asked for yourself? As I mentioned, I was born to a woman who chose not to parent me. I was adopted into a family that, as I grew older, I realized I looked nothing like. Later in life, I realized that we also have quite different energies. My personality is very different from those of my siblings and parents. Although I love my (adoptive) family members very much, I have always felt different from other people because I am different from the people with whom I have my closest relationships.

When I was about five years old, I was out shopping with my grandmother. She ran into a friend, another Jewish woman of similar age. My grandmother introduced me to her friend, and her friend eyed me up and down then remarked, "That's your granddaughter? She looks like a shiksa." Shiksa is a pejorative Yiddish word meaning a non-Jewish woman or girl. I never forgot that exchange. It confirmed for me what I was already thinking and feeling about not fitting in physically with my adopted family. Evidently, I didn't even fit into my community, a predominantly Jewish neighborhood in Baltimore.

I realize now that it was important for me to feel so completely different from my family and community that I looked within for guidance. I learned to trust my own instincts above anyone else's and to think for myself. For that reason I am not a very good follower. I don't necessarily need to lead, either. I don't care who is behind me, if anyone. I just need to be able to go in the direction I think best at the pace I know is right for me. My self-reliance has relieved me of many of the burdens, such as over-identification with tribal beliefs, that typically accompany grounded energy.

I can now see that grounded energy is necessary to accomplish what I am supposed to do in this life. I have been asked to be a guide for channeling in a grounded manner to others who are wired in a similar fashion. To do that, I have to let go of the fear of rejection. That may not have been possible if I had been lovingly raised by my birth parents. Being adopted helped me to develop the skills I needed in order to accomplish the critical things that I came here to do.

Although being adopted can be a difficult experience, it was my own choice made prior to incarnating. Adoption was a necessary part of the psyche for my soul's growth. I had a contract with my birth parents that they were to give me up. My adoptive parents agreed to raise me—also a contract. All of the important relationships in our lives are contracts that were arranged prior to birth. Consider what you have always thought of as negative aspect to your life that may have been your own choices for your soul's evolution.

What aspects of your childhood, your body, or your family of origin have you always wished were different? Although it may be difficult to do so, look at both sides of that coin, positive and negative, and examine how those factors have shaped who you are today.

Try to list issues in your life that you have always wished were different:

1.

2.

3.

4.

5.

Is there a common theme among your five issues? For instance, does each of the five involve a hurt? If that is a theme in your life, what can you learn from those experiences? Forgiveness, perhaps?

If an issue involves a physical attribute, consider what your soul has to gain from incarnating into your current body. For instance, I have often thought that blindness affords those with this condition a higher understanding, the ability to gauge others based on their energy field. Those without eyesight are able to gather information in other ways, such as by engaging their third eye. In addition, they do not have to contend with all of the visual distractions that are always vying for our attention.

For example, I attended a spiritual seminar a few years ago. The lead speaker had invited a guest speaker. Before realizing he was associated with the seminar host, I had already noticed the guest. My lower-chakra response was, That guy's a flake. He had very ungrounded energy. I'm not perfect, folks, as you'll see from the rest of the story.

As a cop for twenty-five years, I acquired the habit of sizing up people and putting them in categories before I know anything about them. Most people do this unconsciously, but cops do it even more. It is a survival mechanism they use to analyze situations quickly. It's also called stereotyping. The problem is that most people don't like to be associated with a stereotype, yet we all do this every day.

Returning to my seminar story, my initial assessment of the guest speaker stayed in effect with no evidence to the contrary at that point. I watched as he approached the author who was holding the seminar. The author addressed the audience, and then introduced this man. I listened to the man speak, trying to make sense of his relationship to the seminar and the esteemed author for whom I had so much respect.

All my questions were quickly answered as this man began to talk about his son, who had been in a car crash the previous year and rendered a quadriplegic. The man went on to say how he was caring for his son, but his son was so angry at the world because of what had happened to him. He said that his son sometimes directs this anger toward him, his most consistent caregiver. The man spoke of this still-very-recent tragedy with strength and conviction. He said he knew that there was a lesson for both him and his son in this turn of events. As he spoke, I realized that my initial assessment of him had been quite wrong. Despite his wispy, long hair and frail appearance, this man emanated a strength more powerful than any well-muscled physique. I was seeing and hearing true inner strength, not physical strength. I thought, This man is beautiful. Then I heard from my spirit guides, "Your eyes will always deceive you."

It was then that I realized our eyes relay information to our brains, which constantly categorize people and events by comparing them to our past relationships and experiences. The conclusions we draw, usually without even being conscious of them, may benefit our physical survival but have the opposite effect on our spiritual evolution. These preconceptions serve to separate us from one another rather than bring us closer together. The inability to see would alleviate that obstacle, although blindness would present a myriad of other challenges.

Have you ever thought of blindness as something positive?

What life circumstances can you reframe to consider from a higher perspective?

What did your mind attach to when you saw this picture?

Chapter 15 Plug-in Points

- Your life is designed by your soul, prior to this incarnation, to meet your spiritual objectives.
- You may have chosen the aspect of your present life you hate the most.
- Common themes in your past-life experiences have embedded lessons.
- Your eyes will always deceive you.
- You can't trust your mind, either.

CHAPTER 16

How Others in Your Life Assist You

"They are your teachers, so be grateful for them."
~ SPIRIT AS CHANNELED BY LESLIE N. BANK

We do not learn much from fun experiences. The same principle applies to learning from interpersonal relationships. Relationships with people of like mind, who have the same background, perspectives, and ideas as us, are not our greatest teachers. These fun relationships just mirror who you think you are back to yourself.

As a police lieutenant, I used to tell my sergeants that their most difficult employees were teaching them how to be better supervisors. I believe that is true from a managerial perspective. I believe it is also true from a human perspective: Our most difficult relationships can teach us the most.

The opportunity for growth and learning in your life exists within your most painful relationships. Take some time to digest this concept. Then try to list five people in your life who cause you pain or conflict.

People/Conflict List:

1.

2.

3.

4.

5.

Look at the people on your list from a higher perspective, and consider what you are learning from these experiences. Consider what they can teach you. Try to assess the situation from a crown-chakra perspective. If it involves a hurt, you usually view it through your fourth chakra, the heart chakra. Instead, try looking at the situation from a crown perspective. In other words, rather than focusing on how you've been hurt, victimized, and so forth, look for the higher lesson that is available to you. Meditate on it if you can. Ask your spirit guides for more information.

Now take the information you've just acquired about the relationship and infuse it with unconditional love for the other person and for yourself. Pray on it. Ask spirit for the strength to view the situation and handle it from a higher perspective. Ask your soul to assist you in your journey to understand the situation.

Write a one- or two-word description of the conflict or issue next to each name on your list. What common themes do you see among these relationships? If there is a common theme, can you accept that the theme is yours and not theirs? For instance, if you have selected three people who do not treat you with respect, can you acknowledge that the issue belongs to you? Consider the possibility that, prior to incarnating, you asked each of these people to help you learn this lesson. Spirit has shown me that the difficult people in our lives are our teachers, not our enemies. Be glad for them and open yourself to the lesson they have to teach.

Your spiritual growth can be compared to bodybuilding and its attempt to increase muscle mass. For muscle size to increase, trauma must occur in the muscle fiber and cause a tear in the tissue. The body then begins to repair this tear by fusing together the muscle fibers with new muscle tissue, increasing the overall size of the muscle. In other words, you must traumatize the muscle to cause the tear which needs repair, which in turn results in the desired larger muscle mass.

As bodybuilders and other athletes recognize, you must consistently challenge your body and its muscles to continue your physical growth. When your physical program is no longer challenging, the routine must be changed if you desire further growth. Without further challenge, you will just maintain what you have. The same is true for growth in other areas of your life.

The difficult people in your life are like a three-hundred-pound weight that's difficult to lift. People and events in your life that offer you resistance are your opportunity to grow stronger. Just like your body handling physical weights, your mind and soul are meant to build up capacity to handle these experiences.

I will offer you an example of growth I obtained from a painful experience. My previous boss, the one with the diamond cross necklace, also hired me after I retired from the police department. She was a friend and mentor at the police department, and I admired and respected her.

When I got my employment offer letter in the mail, the starting annual salary was actually $3,000 more than the figure she and I had agreed upon. I held the letter in my hand and felt an enormous sense of gratitude to her and to spirit for the opportunity. I said to myself, "I will work very hard for her to show her how grateful I am." Spirit then said, "There is something you are going to do for her." I assumed that "something" would be positive.

About a year later, I found myself in a closed-door session with an Equal Employment Opportunity Commission investigator. I was being questioned about my boss's behavior toward another employee. I told the truth about what I had seen and heard; I had no intention of lying. I had become increasingly disappointed in my boss's abusive behavior toward a churchgoing, mild-mannered coworker of mine. I was the first person to give a statement to the investigator. Others, after learning of my statement, opened up about what they had seen and heard. As a result of the investigation, my boss was asked to leave the company or be terminated.

I realized sadly that what I was "doing for her" was to get her fired. From a higher perspective, I saw clearly that there was a lesson for her in the experience, if she chose to learn and grow from it. It was, nevertheless, a difficult experience for all involved. The most painful experiences in our lives offer the most opportunity for growth. It's just that simple.

Your challenge, now that you've reframed your view of the difficult people in your life, is to deal with them using energy from your upper chakras rather than your lower ones. Unconditional love and higher understanding will always bring you the peace you seek.

The Work of Byron Katie, esteemed author and public speaker mentioned in chapter 5, provides four steps for dealing with difficult situations or people. Her perspective and the information provided in her website (www.thework.com) have changed my life. She provides free podcasts, and her videos can be found on YouTube. If you are unable to find peace with someone or something, try doing the four steps of The Work.

Chapter 16 Plug-in Points

- The people in your life with whom you are in conflict are your greatest teachers.
- Look for common themes among your conflict relationships, past or present.
- Your spiritual muscles are like your physical muscles; you need to undergo trauma to achieve growth.
- Be grateful for difficult people. Seek a higher understanding of difficult relationships.
- Go to Byron Katie's website and do The Work for one or more of your difficult relationships.

CHAPTER 17

The Trajectory of Your Life

People want to feel like they are in control of their lives. Some people have even convinced themselves that they are in control of other people's lives. So many of our fears involve a loss of control.

When I began the journey from spiritually unconscious to consciousness, I often lamented that my life had suddenly changed so much and that I missed my old life. Before my life abruptly changed course, I was living in the home I wanted to grow old in, with the woman I wanted to grow old with, and I absolutely loved my job. Everything seemed perfect. I mourned that feeling of perfection, the sense that everything fit in place and was under control, for a long time. In reference to this feeling of loss, spirit said to me, "You cannot possibly know the trajectory of your life. That feeling of control that you once had was and will always be an illusion."

If you don't think that our need to control things exists to create an illusion, consider the people killed in the attacks on September 11, 2001. They left for work on a typical day that quickly became horrifically atypical. We can never know the "trajectory" or path that will be ahead for us. Trajectory is a succinct, perfect word for me (with my police background) to understand, because it is commonly used in forensics for criminal investigations. A trajectory is a mathematically predictable path that an object, such as a bullet, will take after launch. There is no predictable path for any of us, however, regardless of how mundane an existence we have created or how small our world is. If we are meant to experience something, it will come to us.

Chapter 17 Plug-in Points

- People want to feel like they are in control of their lives.
- Control is an illusion that people enjoy to feel safe.
- But you can never know the "trajectory" of your life.
- If you are meant to experience something, it will come to you.

CHAPTER 18

Ego versus Soul

You have two voices within you: your ego and your soul. Your soul, your higher self, contains the wisdom and lessons of all of your previous lifetimes. Your soul knows why you are here and operates on a higher frequency than your ego. Your soul knows that we are all one collective energy from one source.

Your ego, on the other hand, seeks to separate you from the collective. Your ego holds the belief that your tribal group is superior to others. It has its own goals, such as getting that big promotion or your kid making the honor roll. Your ego feels superior to the man on the corner wearing tattered clothes and holding a cup. Your soul knows he is your brother, but your ego is threatened by the soul's voice and seeks to quiet it. Consider this message from spirit about the difference between the two:

There is only one God, although he is called by many different names. No one name is right; He is energy. You each have guides assigned to you. Listen. Quiet your mind. The next voice you hear may not be your own but us trying to speak to you. Slow down. Be still, quiet. Listen. Learn to receive our messages. Meditation is the best way to begin. Your book should contain your personal messages and messages for the masses. We are trying to speak, but only a few can hear. This is why it is important that our words not be kept secret. You are strong. Do not fear their fear. Fear is the weakest of all emotions and should not stop you on your path. Your path is difficult now, but you will soon be walking in sunshine with lush, green grass and birds singing. We will reward you for allowing us to work through you. The rewards will be whatever you want them to be. If it can be done for you, it will manifest, so ask for what you want. You are a beautiful soul with much light and goodness in you. We simply want people to receive their messages. Love above all. Listen to the inner voice that is not in the first person. First person is your human mind. That is the biggest enemy to your evolution. Listen to the other voice. Your human mind may quiet it, thinking the soul's voice to be a threat. The soul's voice tells you to give your lunch to a beggar. Your human mind says he should get a job. See the difference? Your soul's voice is what you must extricate and follow. Find it. Your soul is the source of beauty because it is from God. Your car, house, clothes, the package (body) for the soul are meaningless. Your soul is all that matters, and it is all that continues with you on your journey.

I'm certain that I can't explain it any better than that, so I will end my discussion of the subject with this thought: find your soul's voice, and let it lead you through this life that it has designed. It took some time for me to discern the difference between the two voices, and I still struggle to let my soul have the louder voice. The ego is riddled with fear; the soul is full of faith. Ego wants to compete with other people; the higher self seeks to love others as you love yourself. Once you become familiar with these two levels of thinking, the difference becomes much more distinguishable.

Not only do you have two different voices inside yourself, you also have messages coming in from external sources. Discerning the difference between your higher self and your spirit guides is a little more difficult than distinguishing between ego and soul. There truly is no important difference; whether the information comes from your higher self or from your guides, you should accept it as truth.

Information from your guides will be in the third person, although sometimes my higher self speaks in third person as well. The difference is most apparent when the information is something I could not have known. Also, information from my guides sometimes contains words that I don't normally use and sometimes don't even understand without looking them up. When you have become familiar with how your body responds to receiving the energy of spirit, you will recognize it easily. As discussed in chapters 9 and 11, your physical cue will be something unique to you.

The most important thing is to discern that the information comes from a high level, whether your higher self or spirit. Do not be deceived by your ego. Your ego is full of fear and wants things to remain the same and under the illusion of control. Your ego will give you many reasons why you shouldn't attempt to channel spirit. It will tell you to put this book away and forget about receptivity. It will tell you that people will call you crazy. Your ego is the greatest obstacle in your spiritual evolution. Do not be afraid to find your true voice and let it be heard. Nothing that you aren't prepared for will happen on this journey.

Chapter 18 Plug-in Points

- You have two voices within you: your ego and your soul.
- Your soul, your higher self, contains the wisdom of your previous lives, knows why you are here, and knows that we are all one collective energy from one source.
- Your ego seeks to separate you from the collective and is full of fear; it is threatened by the soul's voice and seeks to quiet it.
- Your ego is your greatest obstacle in your spiritual evolution.
- You must learn to recognize whether information comes from your ego, your higher self, or spirit.

CHAPTER 19

Levels of Spirit

Organizations in both the public and private sectors are arranged in a power hierarchy. Spirit also has a hierarchy with well-defined levels. The difference between levels within a company and the levels of spirit is that a company's hierarchy is based on human power. Human power is rooted in fear and thus has a lower-level frequency. The levels of spirit are based on love and respect, which have a much higher frequency.

The level of spirit closest to your vibration is the category of *peer guides*. These guides are on your evolutionary level. You may have known them in your past lives or they may have existed in your present life but already passed on. They are the lowest level of spirit associated with you.

Instructional guides are at the next level of spirit. They have been assigned to assist you in a specific area of your life. This may be an area in which you have an objective you have had difficulty achieving in your past lives. You chose to obtain some assistance in this life, and these guides agreed to provide the assistance. Some guides come into our lives for a defined period of time, and some are stay with us until we return to their world.

The next level of spirit is the *master spirit* level. Mother Mary, the Buddha, Ganesh, and others are examples of master spirits. The archangels in the Catholic religion would also be in this category. Archangel Michael is a very powerful master spirit. It is my personal belief that Jesus is at the top of the master-spirit hierarchy, somewhere between master spirits and God.

As you might expect, the next—and highest—spirit level is the Supreme Being. A lower-level spirit, let's say a peer guide, will step back if a higher-level spirit wants to speak to you. I was recently channeling and I could see my mother, but she wasn't saying anything. I then realized she was silent because the Blessed Mother was also there. The Blessed Mother has a beautiful energy, yet it feels subtle to me. She just remained there and waited for me to acknowledge and receive her before she spoke. My mother could be present but could not speak while this higher-level spirit had something to say to me. It's just that simple.

The spirit world doesn't involve the ego power structure that exists here on earth. High-level guides receive respect from lower-level guides because they know more and have more information to impart. Many have attained their level by achieving objectives and passing spiritual tests in their past lives. I was once speaking to an instructional guide who was not providing me with clear direction. A master-level guide appeared and gave me the necessary information. The lower-level guide did not seem to have the authority to provide the information I needed. These are just my impressions and experiences; you may have your own which are just as valid.

When you first begin to channel, you will not immediately recognize the different levels of spirit or even to whom you are speaking. When I first started, a spirit guide would appear to me fully. As time went on, however, apparently I was expected to learn their energy signatures, their feeling, to identify them. Now I sometimes glimpse a face or image, but the visuals aren't nearly as clear or long-lasting as they used to be. Sometimes I still ask, "Who is talking to me?" As I explained in chapter 8, you must be sure you are speaking to a spirit of the light. Whenever I ask for clarification, I am given an image. If I get no image or further information, I assume the worst and ask Archangel Michael to keep me safe from whatever is around me.

One last comment: If you are able to connect with any spirit of the light and succeed in receiving information, always end the channeling session by thanking spirit and all of your guides. Guides do not deliver information without higher levels of spirit clearing that information for dissemination. Always express gratitude to all of your guides and to your chosen Supreme Being for interacting with you. It is truly an honor to be visited by these beings.

Archangel Gabriel is known as The Messenger.

Chapter 19 Plug-in Points

- The levels of spirit are based on love and respect. High-level spirit guides receive respect and deference from lower-level guides and they may have more information to impart.
- At the lowest level of spirit, closest to your vibration, are peer guides.
- Instructional guides, assigned to assist you in a specific area of your life, are at the next level of spirit.
- Next are master spirits, including Mother Mary, the Buddha, Ganesh, archangels, and Jesus.
- The highest spirit level is God, the Supreme Being.

CHAPTER 20

Messages from Spirit

"Life is too short to be safe emotionally."
~ SPIRIT AS CHANNELED BY LESLIE N. BANK

received my first channeling message in March 2008. I had asked spirit, "What does the universe want me to know?" I was writing as the answer came through, and this is what I wrote:

The one true thing is love. No one can open you up to more love but you. Love fearlessly, for no one can take anything away from your soul. You are tried and strong. Lessons learned in past lives are renewed and available to you in this life. You are strong and capable of the deepest emotions, a vast range of feelings. You must trust in what you are asked to do and not worry, for we know your limits and will work within them. Love, open more, get help if needed. Open more, live, talk, communicate, love, learn, RISK. Life is too short to be safe emotionally. Life is a lesson, a class, a session to learn, so embrace the teacher. No interaction with another is a waste of time. People will teach you, and you will teach them. LOVE. Risk it. Put all of your chips in the game. You must plant to enjoy the flowers. We love you and are here to help you. We are sorry for your pain. It is fleeting. Teach others as you are being taught. Share these lessons. Live fully. Love fully with no conditions as we love you. Your heart is your lesson. You have conquered courage, strength, and fear. Courage is your forte. Love without hesitation. Do it.

Tears began streaming down my face. Receiving that message was a beautiful experience. The energy from my guides was amazing.

Then I whispered, "But I am afraid."

"You can die in battle; you can risk an emotional wound."

I replied, "Some people are hard to love."

"Love them without terms. That is their purpose in your life. Love them fully. You are learning lessons, and they are your teachers. Be glad for them in your life."

After this channeling session, my life would never be the same. In the beginning, I could only receive while in a meditative state. As I channeled more frequently and the "road" was established, I began to channel information from spirit all the time. Spirit was like a long lost friend I had finally connected with—my spirit guides had much to say! I found their constant chatter distracting at first, so I asked them to slow down in their communications. Since then, I have become accustomed to the honor and privilege of speaking to spirit.

Chapter 20 Plug-in Points

- The one true thing is love. Love fearlessly.
- No interaction with another person is a waste of time. People will teach you, and you will teach them.
- Lessons learned in past lives are renewed and available to you in this life.

CHAPTER 21

Everyday Messages

Not all messages from spirit are repetitive in nature like the injured animals. Sometimes I get a message only once, and usually that happens when I want to learn the higher meaning in a specific experience. This channeling begins with the thought, I wonder what this means? It's really just that simple.

One day, while jogging around a lake in my community, I stopped on a small bridge over a stream. The stream contains runoff that leads from this lake to a larger but less-visited lake nearby. On this occasion, because there had been a severe thunderstorm the night before, there was extra volume in the lake. As a result, the stream was flowing very fast. I looked at the stream and saw a large, black snake feverishly trying to swim upstream in an effort to get back to the smaller lake. That was the only lake the snake knew, the only place he had ever lived. He struggled frantically against the strong current. I watched this process for a few minutes.

I realized that if the snake would just go with the current of the stream, it would eventually end up in a place perhaps even more suited for a snake his size. If he would trust in the process, he would end up in a better place. I also realized that we are all like this snake. We all want to cling to the familiar. We are afraid to go with the current, to trust in the unknown, and to let go of the outcome. The image of this snake and his struggle has stayed with me; it has a larger context. This is an example of one event that you could shrug off or you could consider from a higher level.

At the same lake one Christmas morning, I saw an old woman sitting on a bench alone. The sadness emanating from her being was palpable to me thirty feet away. I sent loving energy to her and heard from spirit, "She is alone because that is how she designed her life." The thought of being a life designer stayed with me for quite a while. I knew this concept had implications for me, as I have hermit-like tendencies. I do not want to be sitting alone on that bench on Christmas morning twenty-five years from now.

Another example of a single message happened one time when I was gardening. I was digging and came across a dead caterpillar. I stared at it and wondered, Why didn't it become a butterfly? I heard the response: "Because he was afraid of change." This message was significant for me, because at the time my life was in extreme upheaval with change all around me. I could either fight the change or trust the process and become something better.

In all these examples of a single message, I had a thought and stayed with it for a moment. In that moment, I did not think anything but instead waited with a clear mind. In that gap between thoughts, spirit sent me a response. You must create a gap in your thoughts to receive a message. My smaller degree of crown energy is a blessing that makes creating a gap in my thoughts easier. But no matter how your energy is distributed, you can practice slowing the pace of your thinking in order to improve your receptivity.

Sometimes, when I'm still, I see the face of someone I knew in this life who has since passed on. Usually I can feel their energy around me. That's my cue that the departed is visiting with me. If I clear my mind, I can then receive their messages. Typically, I will simply say, "Hey, what's up?" They will answer with a sentence or two, sometimes more. Some departed people who I've known come to me routinely; some seldom do. The contact is strictly up to them; with the exception of my adoptive mother, I cannot summon anyone to me. She appears whenever I think about her, which is almost daily. I believe that the departed who visit me are within a range of spirit that I can receive and are typically those with whom I had meaningful relationships in life.

I know one man in spirit who can move physical matter and does so from time to time to let me know he's there. He will move things right in front of me. I don't believe everyone in spirit can do that, but this man is very good at it. I always see his laughing face when I check in to learn more. He is quite a prankster. I recently asked him if he would prank his own kids, to give me a break. He replied that it would only scare them, if they noticed at all. Sometimes being receptive to spirit is like being the only hotel with the vacancy light on—spirits see your light and stop by to visit. I actually really enjoyed this man's energy when he was alive, so I always enjoy his spirit visits, although he can be a bit of a practical joker. He likes to make a big entrance.

If you want to speak with the departed, begin the process by stating that you are open to receiving their messages. Ask them to move something noticeable in your home or to send you a message. When you are in a quiet, peaceful state, if you see in your mind the face of someone you knew who has passed, he or she is visiting with you.

For me, it's never as dramatic as it appears to be on television and movies. It's subtle, except for the practical joker. There's not much subtlety about him, but he is quite endearing.

Note-When I travelled for my work, I found that every hotel had a friendly ghost that would want to initiate contact. My belief is that they just want to connect with you because they know you can. If found myself too tired to engage, I would simply say, "Can you please come back another time? I need to get some sleep". Without exception, this worked. You must let spirit know what you need. If the spirit will not leave your presence, then ask Archangel Michael to assist you in removing this unwelcome spirit from your presence and into the light.

Nothing is random.

Chapter 21 Plug-in Points

- Some messages are "everyday" messages, explanations of the higher meaning in a commonplace event or experience.
- This everyday channeling can begin with the simple thought, I wonder what this means?
- To receive a response from spirit, you must create a gap in your thoughts. To improve your receptivity, you can practice slowing the pace of your thinking.
- You can turn your "vacancy light" off; you do not need to engage with every lonely spirit that seeks contact.

CHAPTER 22

The Dimes

One summer day, my son was riding his bike in the cul-de-sac in front of our home. I stood in front of the house watching him, and I noticed a dime at my feet. I bent down and picked it up; it was very damaged from cars driving over it repeatedly. My son stopped his bike in front of me and asked what I'd picked up. I showed him the dime, and he asked if he could have it. I gave it to him, and he put it in his front pants pocket.

Later that evening, I took the garbage can to the curb. I saw the dime exactly where I had found it and assumed my son had dropped it. It was in the same damaged condition and in the same location. I put it in my pocket and went inside.

When my son got ready for bed and I picked up his pants from the floor, the dime I had given him earlier fell out of his pants pocket. I took the dime I'd just found out of my pocket and examined both dimes: they were in exactly the same condition and had both been found in the same place. I found it odd.

Then I began finding dimes everywhere. I parked my car in a public lot, and two dimes were right outside my car door. There was one under my son's bed. They were simply everywhere. I found about twenty dimes in a two-month period. I realized that finding all of these dimes was beyond coincidence and knew there was a meaning but not what it could be. I asked spirit for guidance and got no response. We only receive guidance when we are meant to.

I was buying a cup of coffee at a local convenience store, and the clerk said, "Can I give you all dimes? We're out of quarters." Okay, I get it, I thought. Dimes had become a joke to me.

I was about to travel to Miami with friends to celebrate my fiftieth birthday. Spirit said to find a dime from each decade of my life within the collection that I'd received. Take a dime from each decade, design a ritual, and then throw them into the ocean during my trip. During the ritual, prior to the dimes' release, ask to be released from old energies that are no longer useful.

Okay, I thought, now I have some idea what the dimes are about. Thank goodness! I met my friends in Miami and performed the ritual as I had been directed.

Across the street from our hotel in Miami, there was a beautiful, old, Spanish church. I usually enjoy visiting churches when I travel, especially older churches. I asked my friends if they would mind checking out the church with me. We had walked across the street and reached the church's marble steps, when my friend JoAnn gasped. She said, "Les, do you see these two dimes?" Two dimes were lying on the steps. I knew at that moment that I would receive guidance in that magnificent church.

We entered the area of worship, and I sat in a pew next to one of my friends. I felt a powerful and very high vibration come into my awareness. I heard, "We are sending someone to you." I was not in a romantic relationship at the time, by choice. I didn't feel ready to be in another relationship yet. I said, "I don't want you to." Then I heard, "Just be open." I knew I would be meeting someone significant soon. Whether I wanted to or not did not matter. My higher self knew what was supposed to happen, but my ego was trying to protect me from being hurt.

Exactly two weeks later, a friend asked me if I was interested in meeting a friend of hers who was single. Like an idiot, despite the information I had been given in the church in Miami, I said no. But then the mutual friend "friended" me on Facebook, and we began talking. When we finally met for a drink, I met a remarkable woman who has been very healing to my heart and soul. I am happy to say I am no longer single and am very lucky to have met her.

I can honestly say that if spirit had not given me this prior information, I probably would have missed out on the opportunity to meet her. Spirit knows me well enough to "prime the pump" to remind me to step outside my comfort zone.

I'm relating this story to show you how spirit works with me. Spirit guides may work with you differently; they want to connect and communicate in whatever manner works for you.

Chapter 22 Plug-in Points

- Spirit guides want to connect and communicate in whatever manner works for you.
- Pay attention to the small things in life—they may be messages from spirit.
- Anything that seems like a coincidence or random is neither and worthy of examination.

CHAPTER 23

Religion versus Spirituality

believe that all religions are like separate roads leading to the same destination. Religions that claim to be the only road and that do not espouse love for all are not the correct path. Although many religions were founded with good intentions, it seems as if religion has done more to separate us than to bring us together.

Although practicing a religion is a good way to begin a dialogue with a higher power, it is not sufficient. For me, religion is a noun. Its repetitive rituals bring people peace in their lives but do not necessarily bring them closer to God. Many people believe that regularly attending religious services allows them to check that box, to be assured their soul will go to a pleasant place when their body ceases to live. I would argue that how you live is far more important than where you spend Sunday morning.

In contrast, I believe spirituality is a verb. Most spiritual people are constantly engaged, always searching for meaning in their lives. Although religion can have a place in your life, there is no separate place for the spiritual aspect of one's self. It is tightly woven into your being, whether you are conscious of it or not. Lighting candles will not, in and of itself, nourish your soul. Singing hymns on Sunday morning cannot replace a true spiritual engagement with your higher power. You're either in or you're out; there is no in-between.

Exploring your soul's purpose and potential is a very private endeavor. You cannot find directions for this journey anywhere but within yourself. Begin this work with a meditation practice. Quiet your mind, and begin to recognize the repetitive patterns of your thinking. Becoming conscious of the inner workings of your mind is the beginning. You can't change what you don't know.

I've given you some tools to work with. It's up to you to decide whether you want to watch from the sidelines or join the game. I hope you will put your fears aside and gear up. Our world needs as many real players as possible on this field.

Chapter 23 Plug-in Points

- All religions are separate roads leading to the same destination.
- Practicing a religion is a good way to begin a dialogue with a higher power, but it is not sufficient.
- Spirituality is constant engagement with your higher power. It is your choice whether to take part.

CHAPTER 24

A Channeled Message for You

Spirit gave me the following message, highlighting the most important teachings from this book, to deliver to you:

As the Buddha taught, everything around you is an illusion. The illusion of your experience is that reality is in the material world. That only the visible is real and only the tangibles are important. One day you will leave your body and all that you possess behind and journey back to your true form. The only things you will bring back with you are the lessons learned, love given and received, and the karma of unresolved transactions. Your house, your car, your hair, your body—these are all temporary and immaterial to your growth. Use this book, these principles, and these methods to break through the illusion of the material world and reconnect with your true purpose. The one common objective for all in body is love. Love one another, accept one another, do not judge one another. Embrace your differences, for all differences are an illusion. You are not different. You are all one collective body from the same source. Violence in word or deed is like suicide; what you do to another you also do to yourself. We love you all and wish you could see yourselves as we see you, as beautiful beings that are inherently perfect. Love is what we want for you to embrace. Love yourself first, and it will be harder to harm others. Love for all is what is needed to ease the tensions in your world. Do not feed hatred with hatred; feed hatred with love. This is a master-level concept that is hard to practice. Begin your spiritual journey with the pace you feel is right. We are here for you, watching you, and ready to guide you.

Chapter 24 Plug-in Points

- Use the teachings from this book to break through the illusion of the material world and reconnect with your true purpose.
- The one common objective for all beings is love.
- Begin your spiritual journey at your own pace.
- Your spirit guides are ready and waiting to guide you.

CHAPTER 25

Workbook

The
Receptivity
Project

This workbook chapter is intended to summarize the main actions recommended in the book.

My energy is. . .

a) stronger above the waist
b) stronger below the waist
c) evenly distributed

Meditation Log

Date	Amount of Time	Impressions
1.		
2.		
3.		
4.		

5.

6.

7.

8.

9.

10.

(This is meant as a template. Continue journaling in a separate notebook.)

Recommended Actions
- Make your home a more comfortable place
    - De-clutter your home
    - Clean your home thoroughly using gentle cleansers
    - Open a pathway to the doors and windows within your home
    - Create a sacred space within your home
    - Research and apply feng shui principles to your home
- Treat your body in a way that will enhance your spiritual receptivity
    - Use crystals, white sage, and essential oils to balance your energy field
    - Adjust your diet to contrast or balance your vibration
    - Quit smoking, reduce or eliminate alcohol, and reduce sugar intake
    - Exercise more frequently
        - If your energy is concentrated above the waist, yoga and calming exercises are best
        - If your energy is concentrated below the waist, aerobic exercise is best
- Attend to your mental and emotional bodily needs
    - Discontinue relationships that do not serve your higher self (toxic, abusive, negative, non-reciprocal, and so forth)
    - Examine your thought processes, weeding out judgment and replacing it with love
    - Meditate to learn more about how your mind works
- Enhance your spiritual bodily needs
    - Begin a daily prayer list
    - Begin a daily gratitude list
    - Examine areas in your life where you have withheld forgiveness
    - Read Byron Katie's teachings and do The Work

- o Consider consulting a hypnotherapist for any necessary healing, which might include a past life regression
- Read spiritual books by metaphysical and spiritual authors to learn more: Pema Chodron, Deepak Chopra, Caroline Myss, Doreen Virtue, Rhonda Byrne, Byron Katie, and Dr. Wayne Dyer
- Find other people on the path of receptivity, by attending group meetings and metaphysical store classes and researching resources on the Internet
- Do the visualization exercises associated with your energy field
- Find a meditation partner with an energy field that will balance yours
- Seek out a spiritual mentor
- Be patient with yourself
- Love yourself

BIBLIOGRAPHY

Burns, David D. *Feeling Good: The New Mood Therapy.* New York: HarperCollins, 2012.

Byrne, Rhonda. *The Power.* New York: Astria Books, 2010.

Byrne, Rhonda. *The Secret.* New York: Astria Books, 2006.

Chodron, Pema. *Comfortable with Uncertainty: 108 Teachings on Cultivating Fearlessness and Compassion.* Boston: Shambhala Publications, 2003.

Chopra, Deepak. *Perfect Health: The Complete Mind/Body Guide* (Revised and Updated Edition). New York: Bantam, 2001.

Hicks, Esther, and Jerry Hicks. *The Law of Attraction: The Basics of the Teachings of Abraham.* Carlsbad, CA: Hay House, 2006.

Katie, Byron. *Loving What Is: Four Questions That Can Change Your Life.* New York: Three Rivers Press, 2003.

McCandless, Cathleen. *Feng Shui That Makes Sense: Easy Ways to Create a Home That FEELS as Good as It Looks.* Minneapolis, MN: Two Harbors Press, 2011.

Myss, Caroline. *Anatomy of the Spirit: The Seven Stages of Power and Healing.* New York: Three Rivers Press, 1996.

———. *Sacred Contracts: Awakening Your Divine Potential.* New York: Three Rivers Press, 2003.

Roman, Sanaya, and Duane Packer. *Opening to Channel: How to Connect with Your Guide.* Tiburon, CA: HJ Kramer, 1993.

Tipping, Collin. *Radical Forgiveness: A Revolutionary Five-Stage Process to Heal Relationships, Let Go of Anger and Blame, and Find Peace in Any Situation.* Louisville, CO: Sounds True, 2010.

Author Biography

Photo courtesy of Wendy Greezicki

Leslie N. Bank retired from the Baltimore Police Department as a lieutenant after serving for nearly twenty-five years, and now works as a security consultant. Bank graduated from Johns Hopkins University with a master of science degree. She lives in Columbia, Maryland, with her eight-year-old son.

A Reiki master, Bank has channeled spirits for about five years, beginning with an extraordinary experience with the spirit realm while meditating. She firmly believes that if she can make this profound connection, other willing people can do so as well.

Made in the USA
Charleston, SC
05 February 2016